THE ARRIVAL OF THE GREEKS

THE EVIDENCE FROM THE SETTLEMENTS

PUBLICATIONS OF THE HENRI FRANKFORT
FOUNDATION

– volume five –

General editor

Jan G. P. Best

THE ARRIVAL OF THE GREEKS

THE EVIDENCE FROM THE SETTLEMENTS

by

René A. van Royen

and

Benjamin H. Isaac

B. R. GRÜNER PUBLISHING CO. — AMSTERDAM
1979

938
R889a

© by B.R. Grüner bv, 1978
ISBN 90 6032 109 X
Printed in The Netherlands

80-10805

FOREWORD

This monograph is the second to result from the University of Amsterdam's research project "The Arrival of the Greeks." The first, "The Arrival of the Greeks," by Jan G.P. Best and Yigael Yadin, Amsterdam 1973, was a publication of the Henri Frankfort Foundation. The project has been led by Jan Best and financially supported by the Netherlands Organization for the Advancement of Pure Research, ZWO. It is thanks to the University and the ZWO that an English translation of this volume has been possible.

The Dutch manuscript of "The Arrival of the Greeks: The Evidence from the Settlements," was completed in July 1976. Preparation of the definitive text owes much to Ine Zantingh, who carefully and critically read each of the many previous versions. The late Mrs. H. Langhout, librarian of the Archaeological Historical Institute, was unusually helpful and unfailingly friendly to our project. The English translation is the work of Bryna Hellman-Gillson, who has provided a text which gives the impression that the authors themselves wrote in English rather than in Dutch.

George Strietman was so kind as to draw Table 3 and all the maps. Hans de Munter made an adaptation of Valmin's general plan.

Emily Vermeule of Harvard University was kind enough to read the English manuscript before publication. Her suggestions for modifications or alterations of the text were gratefully followed, and lacunae and misinterpretations are the sole responsibility of the authors. In principle it has not been possible to include in this study anything published after July 1976.

Inclusion of the appendix "Similar Features in the Architecture of Troy and Malthi Dorion" in this monograph deserves explanation. The appendix was written as a separate study by van Royen alone. It was originally planned to publish it elsewhere but for practical reasons (a.o. the reference made in Best and Yadin 1973: 24 note 33), the study is presented here.

R.A. v. R., Amsterdam University
B.H.I., Tel-Aviv University

CONTENTS

LIST OF ILLUSTRATIONS, MAPS AND TABLES

INTRODUCTION

Few subjects have been so long and so often debated as that of whether the Greeks arrived on the mainland at about 2000 BC or about 1600 BC. The answer to this primarily historical question has been sought primarily in archaeological evidence. But what is the relevant evidence, and what are the principal standpoints taken on it?

Two major cultural transformations mark the Bronze Age on the Greek Mainland. About the beginning of the second millenium before Christ, the Early Helladic culture was replaced by that known as Minyan. Minyan pottery, apsidal houses, cist and tumulus graves distinguish this new culture from its predecessor (Vermeule 1972:66-81). In turn, at about 1600 before Christ, Minyan forms gave way to the pottery styles, shaft and tholos graves and the architecture we now identify as Mycenaean (Vermeule 1972:106-10).

The introduction of Minyan culture and the disappearance of Early Helladic forms is generally accepted to be the result of an Indo-European invasion. In the new edition of "The Cambridge Ancient History," Caskey expresses this opinion: "A new people arrived in central Greece, probably in the twentieth century BC., coming either from the north or the east or both. They spoke an Indo-European language, which either was Greek or was about to become Greek, and one of their technical accomplishments was the making of Minyan pottery, ... In some parts of Greece they settled peacefully in the communities of those who had come before, while elsewhere they captured towns and killed or absorbed the older inhabitants. Before long they were spread through all the Peloponnese and established in the north-west and the north, but the interior parts of Thessaly and Macedonia were never deeply affected by them" (Caskey 1973:139-40).

Changes in material culture around 1600 BC are more difficult to explain. Two partially conflicting opinions exist side by side.

1

The first rejects any influence on Middle Helladic Greece by new immigrants. Cultural transformations, it claims, were the work of the local (Greek) people, at most inspired and stimulated by widening contacts with Cretan and Eastern civilizations. "By the end of the seventeenth century this period of gestation was completing its term and foreign impulses, coming largely from or through the Minoans whose enterprise was potent now in the Aegean, helped to bring forth new interests and ambitions on the mainland ... Princes arose at Mycene, tall powerful men who could organize and lead soldiers and win booty, but there is no compelling reason to suppose that they had come recently from abroad. On the contrary, the mass of evidence suggests that this was a local flowering rather than an interruption ..." (Caskey 1973:140; compare among others Dickinson 1977:107-8, Mylonas 1966:15; Schachermeyr 1968:305; Bengtson 1969:4-6; Marinatos 1973a: 65ff).

The second opinion leaves room for the idea that immigrants from the Near East could have settled in Greece at about 1600 BC. "If they are native Helladic princes, we must account for their new magnificence; if not, we must look for new rulers from some third region; and there are features about the Shaft Graves which at least show that, either way, the area of our inquiry is not to be confined to the Aegean" (Stubbings 1973:633; compare among others Vermeule 1972:108; Best 1973:28; Marinatos 1973b:108-9).

In sum, there is general consensus on two points: that new groups of immigrants did penetrate Greece at about 2000 BC, and that Mycenaean culture after 1600 differs from the earlier, Minyan culture. But there is no consensus of opinion as to whether those differences were the work of the local population or whether immigration again played its significant part. This difference of opinion is of consequence in identifying the bearers of Minyan and Mycenaean culture. If immigration is ruled out, the conclusion must be that the Mycenaeans and these first Greeks of the Minyan period were ethnically one and the same. Conversely, immigration at about 1600 BC would lead to the conclusion that the bearers of Minyan culture and the Mycenaeans who replaced them were not necessarily ethnically alike.

Assuming that the Mycenaeans were Greek and immigration occurred at about 2000 BC but not at about 1600 BC, one would have to conclude that the Greeks first entered Greece at the earlier

2

date. If immigration occurred during both these periods, one would have to conclude that the Greeks entered Greece at the later date and that the immigrants settling there during the period around 2000 BC were not Greek.

As we have said, the primarily historical question of what "happened" in Greece at these two points in time has been, until now, debated in archaeological terms. But an archaeological term does not always refer to a historical fact. All evidence must be interpreted by an archaeologist before it can speak to us, and all archaeologists are influenced by their assumptions. This explains why a particular phenomenon may be interpreted in different ways. An archaeologist's report may also be differently interpreted by other archaeologists. (One example of this is the conflicting interpretation given to Mylonas's report of excavations at Eleusis by Best [Best and Yadin 1973:28 and Schachermeyr 1968:305]).

Interpretation of archaeological material is complex enough at any time, but the question "When did the Greeks arrive?" seems to be more complicated than usual, because it touches a sensitive nerve. There are scholars for whom immigration at about 2000 BC is an acceptable idea but immigration at about 1600 is not. This difference in attitude can easily lead to inconsistent argumentation.

Occurrance or not of immigration cannot easily be established archaeologically. What can be established, however, is the continuity or discontinuity of occupation of settlements. We define "continuity of occupation" as the continuous presence of a group of people at a given place for a length of time which allows the occupants to succeed each other. Disturbances of this pattern, such as the abandonment of the place by its inhabitants or the arrival of immigrants – in either case on an appreciable scale – we define as "discontinuity."

The aim of this study is to gain insight into the extent of (dis-)continuity in the occupation of Greece around 2000 BC and 1600 BC. On the basis of firm criteria for determining continuity and discontinuity respectively, we shall systematically analyze the most important archaeological material from these two periods. The same criteria will be used to analyze all material, so that if evidence A leads to interpretation B, that interpretation must be deduced from all cases of evidence A, regardless of the period to which they are assigned.

Houses and settlements are by far the most suitable evidence for such a study. Provided the stratigraphic environs of a house have not been destroyed, we can ascertain when it was built, how long it was occupied, if and when it was renovated or reconstructed. Since graves, pottery deposits and isolated finds provide less exact evidence, we have not included such phenomena in our study.

Only if a house or settlement can be accurately dated can the history of its occupation be analyzed. Thus we have found that the vague dating "2000 BC and 1600 BC" is not precise enough for this study. Instead we shall speak of "transitional periods": EH II/EH III, EH III/early MH and late MH/LH I. The term "transitional period" is used in a strictly chronological sense; the end of EH II and the beginning of EH III form the transitional period EH II/EH III. It should not be interpreted as referring to an interval between EH II and EH III.

These sub-divisions of the Bronze Age have become the accepted system of dating since the publications of Caskey (1960), Buck (Buck 1964 and Dickinson 1977:71) and Dickinson (1974 and 1977). Each of the periods is delineated by the appearance, use and disappearance of distinct and recognizable types of pottery. Characteristic of the EH II period is the so-called sauceboat, which was no longer made during the EH III period, when the so-called tankard and the first grey Minyan ware were in use. The beginning of the MH period is marked by the appearance − or continued use − of grey Minyan ware in combination with matt-painted pottery and the disappearance of the tankard found at EH III sites.

Division of the MH period is not as exact. Buck speaks of an early and a later phase, a division which Dickinson agrees is applicable to most of the area we include in this study (Dickinson 1977:17).

Difficulties arise when dating the beginning of the LH I period. Dickinson discerns differences between Aegean imported pottery from late MH and genuinely LH I pottery (Dickinson 1977:22 and 25), and believes that this can be justified by certain distinct characteristics (Dickinson 1977:25 ev.). It is not important to this study to go into the question of differences between Vapheiocups dated late MH and Vapheiocups dated LH I. We shall accept as LH I pottery all that displaying the characteristics named by Dickinson.

Since significant pottery is the most exact method of dating available to us, we shall pay particular attention to its presence at the sites under consideration in this study.

4

As we have said, the aim of this study is to discover the extent of continuity and discontinuity in the occupation of settlements around the dates 2000 BC and 1600BC, which fall within the periods EH II/EH III, EH III/early MH and late MH/LH I. Distinct types of pottery have been assigned to each of these periods which, when found in conjunction with identifiable architectural remains, tell us whether the houses which stood there were lived in during more than one period and whether, during that time, they were rebuilt, destroyed or abandoned. A house in which one finds late MH pottery on a lower level and LH I pottery on a higher level can be said to have been lived in continually during the transitional period late MH/LH I. In this study we shall analyze how many settlements in Greece show evidence of continuity and discontinuity during the three transitional periods, and to what degree.

Our study will begin with an inventory of the settlements at which identifiable architectural remains from the relevant periods have been discovered. Only a few of the EH and MH sites discussed in available surveys can be so analyzed (Ålin 1962, Hope Simpson 1965, Syriopoulos 1964, 1968, Schachermeyr 1971, 1974, and later short reports in AA, AAA, AD, BCH and Ar.R.).

Our next step will be to ascertain whether sufficient material is available for accurate dating and a continuity/discontinuity analysis of the architectural remains. An uninformative report on an excavation, even where significant pottery has been found, or disturbed stratigraphy hinder a continuity/discontinuity analysis. Such sites can be found in the chapter "Other Sites."

All sites which lend themselves to it will then be analyzed for their pattern of continuity or discontinuity of occupation. The degree of (dis)continuity will be assessed as follows:

1. Conclusive evidence of continuous occupation — Stratified remains indicate the introduction of a new culture without coincident signs of destruction, abandonment or removal of the settlement to another site. Abrupt changes in the size or structure of the settlement, that is: enlargement or reduction of the built-up area or shift of its center, are also not evident.

2. Evidence of continuity of — Stratified remains indicate the intro-

5

occupation but with traces of discontinuity:

duction of a new culture without coincident signs of major destruction. There are, however, traces of partial damage (perhaps subsequently rebuilt on site) or temporary abandonment or removal of the settlement. There may also be signs of abrupt but minor enlargement or reduction of the built-up area or slight displacement of its center.

3. Evidence of discontinuity of occupation, though with traces of continuity:

Despite traces of continuity, there is strong evidence, in stratified remains laid down during the introduction of a new culture, of major though incomplete destruction (whether or not subsequently rebuilt on new sites), abandonment, displacement or sudden and extensive enlargement or reduction of the built-up area, or a more than slight displacement of its center.

4. Conclusive evidence of discontinuity of occupation:

Clearest evidence is the founding of a new settlement on previously unbuilt or abandoned ground during a period of cultural transformation. Other examples are destruction or mass abandonment of the settlement (with or without rebuilding in a different architectural style), or a shift in site of the whole settlement.

The values 1, 2, 3 and 4 indicate the level of (dis)continuity, and these values can be found in our analysis by site and on our maps and tables.

Finally it must be said that the aim of this study necessitates a strictly comparative method. This means that we must confine ourselves to those areas in which EH, MH and LH cultures flourished, and where finds of the same pottery types give us the greatest possible chance to date the sites precisely. These areas are: Argolis, Corinthia, Arcadia, Laconia, Messenia, Elis, Achaia, Attica and Aegina, Boeotia, Phocis and Euboea. Excluded therefore are:

6

Aetolia, Acarnania, the Ionian Islands, Locris and Spercheios Valley and Malis, since Mycenaean culture was introduced here late in the LH period. Thessaly must also be excluded, though LH I remains have been unearthed there, as it is not possible to speak of an EH culture in that area (see page 35).

We shall begin with a continuity/discontinuity analysis of the relevant sites for the period about 2000 BC — the transitional periods EH II/EH III and EH III/early MH, and will then go on to analyze the period about 1600 BC — transitional period late MH/ LH I. A short discussion of sites in these areas which do not lend themselves to a continuity/discontinuity analysis will follow under the heading "Other Sites." The chapter "Conclusions" which contains maps and tables closes this study. An explanation of the "Appendix" can be found in the foreword.

ANALYSIS OF THE TRANSITIONAL PERIODS EH II/EH III
AND EH III/EARLY MH

ARGOLID:

Significant architectural remains have been attested in Tiryns, Argive Heraeum, Berbati, Palaiokastro near Dendra, Argos, Lerna, Asine, Synoro, Kandia, Phlius and Spetsai. It has only been possible in the cases of Tiryns, Berbati, Argos, Lerna and Asine to make use of our specified criteria for analyzing continuity/discontinuity. All other places have been relegated to the chapter "Other Sites."

TIRYNS:

Traces of Early and Middle Helladic settlements were found by Müller at the upper, middle and lower palaces of Tiryns. EH construction at the upper and middle palaces had been destroyed by fire: "Der Rundbau (tholos) is durch Feuer zerstört, gewiss in demselben Brande, der auch das Haus östlich davon, von dem wir nur einen Magazinraum kennen, vernichtet hat, und dem auch auf der Mittelburg mehrere Häuser dieser Periode zum Opfer gefallen sind. Es kann sein, dass die ganze Siedlung in diesem Brande zu Grunde ging" (Müller 1930:203).

With regard to dating this catastrophe, he notes: "Der Rundbau ist älter (that is: than the transitional period EH/MH), gehört also zweifellos noch in frühhelladische Zeit, wenn auch nicht in deren älteste Tirynther Phase" (Müller 1930:87). Destruction of the tholos has been more precisely dated by Caskey on the basis of pottery remains as being at the end of the EH II period (Caskey 1960:300-1). Recent excavations in the area of the lower palace have corroborated this dating: "Die Brandschicht Θ 1, die noch an mehreren Stellen in den Schnittwänden der nordwestlichen Unterburg sichtbar ist und von der auch noch einige kleine Stege im Bereich der Abschnitt II/2 stehen, lässt sich stratigrafisch mit den Brandschichten frühhelladischer Zeit verbinden, die K. Müller

auf der Ober- und Mittelburg festgestellt hat ... Die Zerstörungs-
schichten markieren ... den Ubergang von FH II zu FH III, ..."
(Siedentopf 1971:84-5 and Grossmann 1971:63 note 120). Unfortunately, the transitional period EH III/early MH in Tiryns has
not been completely investigated, and even recent findings have
given us no decisive answers (Voigtländer 1973:30).

Conclusion: Burnt debris over a large area is evidence of discon-
tinuity of occupation.
EH II/EH III: 4
EH III/early MH: inconclusive

ARGOS:

Excavations on Aspis, in Deiras and at other sondages in the area
around the present city give us information about occupation
patterns in Argos during the Bronze Age. No EH material was
found under the remains of the MH settlement on Aspis (Vollgraff
1906:6-7, 1907:139). Besides an MH house, a number of other
sunken constructions of the MH period have been excavated within the Deiras necropolis (Daux 1959:770; Deshayes 1966:15-21,
235-8). Within the city limits of Argos, MH material comprising
pottery and correlated architectural remains have been found to
lie immediately above virgin soil: S 86 (Daux 1969:1017), Su 74
(Daux 1967:808), Sondage 67 (Daux 1959:755), in the grids BQ
54/55 (Bommelaer and Grandjean 1971:736), BA 33, BB 33, AZ
34, BA 34 (Bommelaer and Grandjean 1971:746), AX 29, BA 33
(Daux 1969:986), BA 32 (Croissant 1972:884) and in the Quartier
Sud (Daux 1956:370).

Middle Helladic material has been located directly above neo-
lithic strata in the grids BF 8, BE 7, BE 8 (Daux 1967:817-8).
Material which can definitely be dated early MH has been unearthed
in the sondages S 86 (Daux 1969:1019), Su 74 (Daux 1967:808),
BF 8, BE 7, BE 8 (Daux 1967:817). Since the earliest Bronze Age
material attested here can be dated early MH, we must conclude
that a settlement was founded at Argos at the beginning of the MH
period.

Conclusion: Founding of a new settlement is evidence of discontinuity of occupation.
EH III/early MH: 4

9

LERNA:

The stratigraphy of the EH settlement at Lerna is one of the best preserved and investigated in all Greece. Strata relevant to our study are Lerna III, IV and V. Lerna III is accepted as being contemporary with EH II, Lerna IV with EH III and the beginning of Lerna V as coeval with the first phase of MH. Caskey summarizes the transformation from Lerna III to Lerna IV as follows: "The burning of the House of the Tiles marked the end of Period III, and marked it very clearly indeed, both historically and archaeologically ... The debris of the destruction can be distinguished with certainty from the remains of the succeeding settlements ... The place of the great building was then set aside through the forming of a low round tumulus over its ruins" (Caskey 1960:293). The earliest apsidal house at Lerna IV was "... so placed that it overlay the eastern end of the House of the Tiles and just touched the circle of the tumulus" (Caskey 1960:294). The destruction by fire of the House of the Tiles and the construction of an apsidal house over a section of its ruins mark the transition in Lerna from EH II to EH III.

With regard to the transition from Lerna IV to Lerna V, Caskey noted: "It is enough to bear in mind that there was no evidence of break or interruption in the sequence of habitations." This is evident from the lack of burnt debris and the unchanging orientation of later apsidal houses (Caskey 1966:150).

Conclusion: Destruction of important buildings by fire and re-orientation of new buildings is evidence of discontinuity of occupation. Unchanged orientation of new construction during EH III/ early MH and lack of burnt debris is evidence of continuity of occupation.

EH II/EH III: 4
EH III/early MH: 1

ASINE:

Of the excavations on the acropolis, the stratigraphy of the large trench in the Lower City is the most important for our study. The excavators have the following to say: "At a depth of 260-270 cm. below the Late Mycenaean level the transition from MH to EH is marked by a thick burnt layer, ..., with a hole for a post which supported the roof of the latest EH III building, the one destroyed by fire" (Frödin and Persson 1938:202). Relating EH strata in

10

Asine to the Lerna chronology, Caskey writes: "The excavators called this level Early Helladic III, noting the features similar to those at Zygouries. It should now be recognized, I think, as a characteristic settlement of Early Helladic II. All the pottery ... is of types that occur exclusively in Period III at Lerna" (Caskey 1960:301; compare Frödin and Persson 1938:221-3 with Caskey 1960:286-293).

Caskey's conclusion, then, is that Asine was destroyed by fire in the period Asine EH III = Lerna III = EH II, contemporaneously with Lerna and other settlements in the Argolid. Evidence on strata in Asine, which correspond to EH III and early MH levels, are inconclusive. Recent excavations have not changed this picture (Michaud 1973:299; Michaud 1974:607, Catling 1973/74:11).

Conclusion: The layer of burnt debris dated EH II is conclusive evidence of complete destruction and consequently of discontinuity of occupation. Such evidence is lacking for the transitional period EH III/early MH.

EH II/EH III: 3
EH III/early MH: inconclusive

BERBATI:

Of Bronze Age remains investigated at the Mycenaean necropolis and on the southern and eastern slopes of the acropolis at Berbati, only the settlement found on the southern slope is of importance. with regard to the transition EH II/EH III here, the excavators have pointed out: "There was no positive evidence of a catastrophic destruction of the Megaron, but the complex seems to have ceased to have been inhabited before EH III. This may also be inferred from the fact that the EH III building N intersects the wall a^V, which belongs to the eastern annexe of the megaron" (Säflund 1965:101). This pithos store N was built and remained in use during EH III (Säflund 1965:130).

The transitional period EH III/early MH, however, shows clearer signs of discontinuity of occupation: "On the other hand, the buildings of the intermediate period between EH and MH (EH III) in this part of the hillslope were destroyed by a large fire ..." (Säflund 1965:101). Recent excavations have not altered these impressions (Schachermeyr 1971:389).

Conclusion: Minor displacement of houses within the built-up area during the period EH II/EH III is evidence of continuity of

11

occupation with traces of discontinuity. The great fire on the southern slope at the end of EH III is conclusive evidence, in our opinion, of discontinuity of occupation.

EH II/EH III: 2
EH III/early MH: 4

CORINTHIA:

Significant architectural remains are attested in Zygouries, Corinth, Korakou, Gonia, Perachora and by Lake Vouliagméni (Perachora). Only in the case of Zygouries is it possible to assess continuity/discontinuity according to the given criteria. All other places will be found in our chapter headed "Other Sites."

ZYGOURIES:

For dating the transition from EH to MH on the hill at Zygouries, we have the following material: a large number of EH dwellings which could be dated by pottery found on site have been excavated in the central area of the hill. Architectural remains and correlated pottery from the MH period, however, have not been found. The opinion of the excavator is that the dwellings found in the upper EH stratum were destroyed by fire: "The flourishing village at Zygouries, which may be taken to represent the final stage reached after many centuries in the slow progress of Early Helladic civilization, appears to have been abruptly destroyed by fire" (Blegen 1928:221), and this last phase he dates in the period EH III (Blegen 1928:220).

Pottery remains found in these fire-destroyed houses are, in the main, identical with those from Lerna III. Caskey noted: "The representative group of houses at Zygouries, ..., yielded very large quantities of pottery and other objects like those which are now paralleled at Lerna III" (Caskey 1960:300). The "sauceboat" characteristic of EH II was found in nearly every house (Blegen 1928:8, 9, 12, 18, 20, 22, 23, 25, 27; figs.: 78-81). Caskey concluded that Zygouries was destroyed by fire in the final phase of EH II rather than at the end of EH III (Caskey 1960:301), and this implies that the transition EH III/early MH — as in the case of Asine — must be looked for in the so-called MH strata. Despite evidence of MH construction on bed-rock (Blegen 1928:3), there is not enough material here to justify an opinion.

Conclusion: Destruction over a large area at the end of EH II is conclusive evidence of discontinuity of occupation. Evidence is lacking for the period EH II/early MH.

EH II/EH III: 4
EH III/early MH: inconclusive

ARCADIA:

Architectural remains of some interest are attested in Asea and Pheneos. Only in the case of Asea is it possible to assess continuity/discontinuity according to the given criteria. Pheneos will be found in our chapter headed "Other Sites."

ASEA:

Excavations in the central area of the hill at Asea give us the most information. With regard to the transition EH/MH the excavator noted: "The youngest houses from this period (i.e. EH) have all been destroyed by fire, and over the entire plateau a thick ash-layer forms the boundary between this period and the next" (Holmberg 1944:11). Since, in recording the excavation at Asea, the terms EH I, II and III were not used in the same manner as is currently accepted (Caskey 1960:300), we must attempt a translation of the evidence.

Dwellings A and K belong to the earliest group of houses from the EH period which were destroyed by fire. A "sauceboat" of type Lerna III was found under the layer of ashes in house A (Holmberg 1944:12, fig. 73), and this means that house A − and also house K which was contemporaneous − must be dated at the end of EH II (cf. Caskey 1960:301). Thus, this layer of ash overlying the entire plateau may also confidently be dated to the same period.

On the basis of Holmberg's publication, there is nothing useful to be said about the architecture of a possible EH III stratum. At best, the absence of Mattpainted ware in the lowest MH level (Holmberg 1944:97) indicates that there may be an EH III stratum to be found in Asea.

Conclusion: A considerable layer of burnt debris over a wide area − "the entire plateau" − is conclusive evidence of discontinuity of occupation.

EH II/EH III: 4
EH III/early MH: inconclusive

LACONIA:

The survey by Waterhouse and Hope Simpson gives evidence of a large number of probable settlements in Laconia of the EH/MH period. Writing of those settlements where considerable architectural remains have been excavated, the authors report: "No Early Helladic settlement in Laconia has yet been fully excavated, although EH levels have been found at Kouphovouno, the Amyklaion and Geraki" (Waterhouse 1961:168 note 299). However, the excavations at Kouphovouno have not yet been published (Waterhouse 1960:72), EH/MH remains of dwellings have not been found at Geraki (Waterhouse 1960:86), and EH architectural remains are absent in the Amyklaion (Buschor 1927:4). Recent excavations on Kythera have also brought no EH/MH architectural remains to light (Coldstream 1972:272).

Since 1961 architectural remains of significance have been attested in Pavlo Petri and Aghios Stephanos. Only in the case of Aghios Stephanos is it possible to assess continuity/discontinuity according to the given criteria. Pavlo Petri will, therefore, be found in our chapter headed "Other Sites."

AGHIOS STEPHANOS:

Taylour's excavations on the hill at Aghios Stephanos have given us some information about habitation during the EH/MH period there. The most important EH remains have been found in area A and to a lesser extent in area Δ. Writing of the successive stages of occupation in area A, Taylour comments: "In the area A, the pottery found with the burials and in the settlement shows that occupation was widespread in the EH period, during which there seem to have been two building phases; but EH III pottery does not appear to be represented and the site must have been abandoned during that phase" (Taylour 1972:261). New excavations have confirmed this assumption: "Five new trenches were opened on the south side of the hill. EH II occupation deposits were found immediately above bed-rock. Over this horizon there was normally a complete MH sequence; no trace has yet been found of an EH III deposit" (Catling 1973/74:15).

Conclusion: Absence of an EH III stratum is conclusive evidence of discontinuity of occupation during the transitional period EH II/EH III. The founding of an MH settlement is also clear evidence of discontinuity of occupation.

14

EH II/EH III: 4
EH III/early MH: 4

MESSENIA:

A comprehensive picture of Helladic settlements in Messenia has been available to us since the publication of the surveys carried out by the Minnesota expedition (McDonald and Rapp 1972). Although our study must confine itself to evidence supplied by remains of dwellings which can be correlated with distinctive pottery, the general observations made by McDonald and Hope Simpson about settlements in Messenia during the periods EH II/EH III, EH III/early MH and late MH/LH I (McDonald and Rapp 1972:131-42) cannot be ignored (see infra p. 22-3).

Remains of settlements of some importance have been attested in Malthi (McDonald and Rapp 1972:296 # 222), Nichoria (McDonald and Rapp 1972:280 # 100) and Akovitika (McDonald and Rapp 1972:290 # 151). However, it is not possible in these three cases to assess continuity/discontinuity according to our criteria. Discussion of these three settlements will be found in our chapter "Other Sites."

ELIS:

Since the survey work done by Sperling (McDonald 1942), Meyer (Meyer 1957), McDonald and Hope Simpson (McDonald and Hope Simpson 1961, 1969) and the Minnesota expedition (McDonald and Rapp 1972:300-8; register nrs. 244-332 referring to Elis), the existence of a number of probable EH/MH settlements has been recognized. For general observations on the importance of the McDonald and Rapp publication about Elis, see infra p.22-3 Significant architectural remains have only been attested for Olympia in both the Altis (McDonald and Rapp 1972:304 # 315) and near the New Museum (McDonald and Rapp 1972:306 # 321). In neither case, however, is it possible to analyze continuity/discontinuity. For comments on these sites, see our chapter "Other Sites."

ACHAIA:

Examination of EH/MH settlements in Achaia is at the moment in a preliminary stage which makes an assessment of continuity/discontinuity according to our criteria impossible. Information on

15

the present state of work at these sites can be found in our chapter "Other Sites."

ATTICA AND AEGINA:

Significant architectural remains have been found in Aghios Kosmas, Brauron, Thorikos, Rafina, Askitario, Marathon, Eleusis, and near the Aphrodite temple on Aegina. Only in the case of Aghios Kosmas and Eleusis have we been able to assess continuity/discontinuity. All other sites will be found under "Other Sites."

AGHIOS KOSMAS:

Traces of an important EH settlement have been excavated on Cape Aghios Kosmas (Mylonas 1959). According to the excavator, two EH phases, Aghios Kosmas I and II, can be distinguished. Of Aghios Kosmas I, on its bed-rock foundation, there remains unfortunately too little architectural evidence (Mylonas 1959:12). Architectural remains from Aghios Kosmas II are more extensive (Mylonas 1959:20). According to Mylonas: "Aghios Kosmas was destroyed violently by fire ... Again the layer of sand found over the Early Helladic strata will indicate that the site remained unoccupied after the destruction of Aghios Kosmas II, i.e. during the Middle Helladic period" (Mylonas 1959:149).

On the basis of an exhaustive discourse in which he includes stratigraphic evidence from other EH sites with pre-Caskey chronology, Mylonas concludes that this destruction and abandonment must be dated at the end of EH III (Mylonas 1959:157-61).

The absence of typical EH III pottery, such as tankards and (Argive) patterned ware, and the number of "sauceboats" found in the fire-ruined houses of Aghios Kosmas II (Mylonas 1959:26-48), make Caskey's correction more acceptable: that is, Aghios Kosmas II = EH II (Caskey 1960:300). Acceptance of this dating means that the assumed lack of dwellings during the MH period must also apply to the EH III period.

Conclusion: Destruction by fire of a large number of houses, followed by complete abandonment of the settlement, is evidence of discontinuity of occupation.

EH II/EH III: 4

EH III/early MH: not relevant

16

ELEUSIS:

Remains of an MH settlement have been excavated in Eleusis (Mylonas 1932). Fragments of EH pottery were found but no evidence of an EH settlement came to light (Mylonas 1932:151). This means that any EH settlement which might have existed in this area would have to have been located elsewhere. Mylonas distinguished two separate phases, early and late, in the settlement which he uncovered here (Mylonas 1932:151). The early settlement comprised dwellings built on bed-rock: " Ὁ πρῶτος μεσοελλαδικὸς συνοικισμὸς ἦτο ἱδρυμένος ἐπὶ τοῦ βραχοῦ ἤτοι δὲν ἱδρύθη ἐπὶ τῶν ἐρειπίων προγενεστέρου χωρίου" (Mylonas 1932:151).

This early MH stratum is characterized by apsidal houses (Mylonas 1932:5, fig. 151), grey and black Minyan ware (Mylonas 1932:13) and early Mattpainted pottery (Mylonas 1932:13; compare Buck 1964:282). The combination of all this evidence leads inescapably to the conclusion that a completely new settlement was established on bed-rock at Eleusis at the beginning of the MH period.

Conclusion: New building is evidence of discontinuity of occupation.

EH II/EH III: not relevant
EH III/early MH: 4

BOEOTIA:

Significant architectural remains of pre-Mycenaean Bronze Age settlements in Boeotia have been attested in Thebes, Dramesi, Orchomenos, Chaeronea, Lithares and Eutresis. Remains of dwellings found in Dramesi, Orchomenos and Chaeronea cannot be fitted into the presently accepted chronology for EH/MH periods, and the sites excavated at Lithares and Thebes have been, until now, too narrow in scope to be useful to this study. These sites can be found in our chapter "Other Sites."

EUTRESIS:

The most important area excavated on the hill at Eutresis is near the mediaeval tower, where notable EH and MH architectural remains have been uncovered (Goldman 1931:plans). The transition from EH II to EH III shows no trace of discontinuity of habitation according to our criteria (Goldman 1931:20-1, 229).

17

But the EH III settlement ceased to exist after an extensive fire: "The Early Helladic period ends with the destruction of some house walls and with a catastrophic fire which was most devastating on the western side of the summit but was everywhere apparent, except in Pit V where there were no signs of conflagration" (Goldman 1931:231). The existence of an EH III settlement and its destruction by fire is borne out by Caskey's later excavations: "A layer of burnt debris, which had been recorded by the earlier excavators as overlying the remains of EH III in almost all parts of the site, was clearly observable in Trench B" (J.L. Caskey and E.G. Caskey 1960:167).

Given our criteria for establishing continuity/discontinuity of occupation, it is furthermore of importance that houses of a new type were built over this layer of debris (Goldman 1931:231), and that trial trenches proved that the built-up area of the MH settlement was smaller than that of the EH III settlement (Goldman 1931:31).

Conclusion: Lack of signs of destruction indicate continuity of occupation during EH II/EH III. Later destruction by fire and subsequent rebuilding in a different architectural style and on an obviously reduced area are conclusive evidence of discontinuity of occupation during EH III/early MH.

EH II/EH III: 1
EH III/early MH: 4

PHOCIS:

Of pre-Mycenaean Bronze Age settlements in Phocis, only Kirrha, Krisa and Aghia Marina offer attested architectural remains of any significance. Since it has not been possible to date the remains from the Magoula at Aghia Marina (Sotiriadis 1912) within the framework of the EH/MH chronology, we must eliminate this site from our survey. Krisa will be found in the chapter "Other Sites."

KIRRHA:

Excavations on the Magoula at Kirrha uncovered substantial EH architectural remains. The excavators distinguished two distinct phases of the EH III period: HA IIIa and B (Dor and others 1960:30). It was at the end of this HA IIIb phase that habitation here was fundamentally disturbed: "A la fin de la même époque,

18

par contre, on constante un profond bouleversement: la poterie protohelladique très caractéristique disparaît totalement; une épaisse couche de terre mêlée de charbons, de cendres et d'arguile cuite s'étend sur le site ..." (Dor and others 1960:30). Thus the excavators had reason to assume discontinuity of habitation. Caskey, however, using the pottery sequence established at Lerna, correct their chronology, so that Kirrha HA IIIa and IIIb = EH II, and the strata immediately above must be dated Kirrha HM Ia = EH III and Kirrha HM Ib = early MH. Caskey also considered it likely that the burnt stratum of which Dor writes corresponds chronologically with the same evidence at the end of Lerna III = EH II (Caskey 1962:211). This layer, of which Caskey speaks, is to be seen in pit 1 of the section (Dor and others 1960: plate IV).

But neither Caskey nor the excavators at Kirrha placed any special emphasis on the signs of conflagration found under the stratum Kirrha HM 1b = early MH in two of the five pits. In pit 1 whitish ash and in pit 5 red-burned loam were found between the EH III and early MH niveaux (Dor and others 1960: plate IV). We believe, therefore, that equally strong evidence exists for destruction by fire at the end of EH III as for a destruction at the end of EH II.

Later excavations have not changed this picture (Nikopoulou 1968, Petrakos 1973).

Conclusion: Taking into account the section drawing for Kirrha, we must conclude that partial destruction occurred during the transitional period EH II/EH III and that more extensive but still partial destruction took place during the transitional period EH III/early MH.

EH II/EH III: 2
EH III/early MH: 3

EUBOEA:

Although a large number of probable Bronze Age settlements are known to have existed in this region (Sackett a.o. 1966), architectural remains have come to light only near Manika and Lefkandi (Xeropolis). Unfortunately, evidence from excavations in Manika could not be included in this study, as the relevant publication (Theochares 1959:292-306) was not available to the authors. Lefkandi will be found in the chapter "Other Sites."

19

ANALYSIS OF THE TRANSITIONAL PERIOD
LATE MH/LH I

Until now, we have analyzed continuity/discontinuity with the help of distinctive pottery associated with architectural remains, since certain types, or combinations of types, of pottery can date accurately enough for our purposes the architectural remains with which they are associated. House walls and "sauceboat" fragments found together under a layer of ash indicate destruction at the end of EH II, and Grey Minyan and early Mattpainted coarse ware lying together on the floor of an apsidal house date the site to early MH.

The dating of MH architectural remains is, unfortunately, not so simple. A straightforward correspondence such as "sauceboats" equals EH II has not yet been established for the MH period. On this point Buck comments: "The Middle Helladic strata of the various sites are divided into two or three phases dependent upon local variations. Thus the MH II phase at Korakou does not correspond with the MH II phase at Asine and neither of these with MH II at Kirrha" (Buck 1964:281).

Buck goes on to suggest a rough, provisional classification within the MH period: "... it is possible to make a division between the levels where Grey and Argive Minyan, Red Monochrome, and Mattpainted Coarse Ware predominate, and those where Yellow Minyan, Mattpainted Polychrome, and Mattpainted Fine Wares occur frequently. The lower levels might be termed MH I and the upper MH II" (Buck 1964:282). Use of the term "late pottery" in this study refers to Buck's classification "MH II pottery."

Dating with pottery in the LH I period is a simpler matter: both form and decoration of ceramics are distinctive to the LH I period and easily distinguished from LH II and later wares. We have accepted as LH I pottery the ceramic evidence so-called in Dickinson's recent study LH I (= LH I A) (Dickinson 1974).

On the basis of this division, it should be possible to date architectural remains to late MH or LH I and to go on to analyze for abandonment, re-building and so on. Unfortunately, in too many cases, LH I and late MH pottery remains have been found together in one stratum, leading some experts to speak of an MH/LH transitional period preceding the true Helladic period. The assumption is illogical: if a television set is found in a centuries-old farm house, we can say that the house was occupied as late as the era of television but not that television dates back to the time the house was first built. Just so, MH pottery found in conjunction with LH I pottery must have been preserved and used into the later period, and LH I pottery cannot be dated earlier when it is found together with MH pottery.

In sum, we have assumed as a basis for this study that a combination of late MH and LH I pottery evidence dates the associated architectural remains to LH I, and that purely late MH pottery finds date the associated architectural site to late MH.

ARGOLID:

Significant architectural remains have been attested in Mycenae, Tiryns, Argos, Lerna and Asine. It has been possible only in the case of Argos to make an assessment of continuity/discontinuity with our specified criteria. Other places have been relegated to our chapter "Other Sites."

ARGOS:

Extensive MH building has been attested in Argos but on only one site was it followed by LH architecture. Near the Aphrodision, a trench at grave T 301 revealed several MH niveaux, the uppermost of which is contemporary with the nearby grave. "Un sol de terre battue et de petits cailloux, conservé sur une surface restreinte à l'O. de la tombe T 301 (fig. 6), paraît correspondre à une dernière phase d'occupation, ..., et contemporaine de la tombe" (Daux 1969:989). Both the grave and the coeval floor niveau could be dated to the last phase of the MH period by the Mattpainted fine ware goblet found on site.

Architectural remains immediately above this late MH stratum date from the LH III C period or slightly earlier (Daux 1969:992). The evidence makes it possible to accept the excavators' conclusions: "C'est après une période d'abandon assez longue que est venu s'installer, sur les ruines méso-helladiques, l'habitat mycé-

21

nien" (Daux 1969:991). Later excavations have not altered this picture (Croissant 1972:884; Michaud 1974:761).

Conclusion: Abandonment of a late MH settlement is evidence of discontinuity of habitation.

Late MH/LH I: 4

CORINTHIA:

Significant architectural remains have been attested in Zygouries, Korakou, Gonia and Nemea. Following our criteria it has not been possible to analyze any of these sites for continuity/discontinuity, and they can be found in our chapter "Other Sites."

ARCADIA:

The architectural remains attested in Asea and Pheneos do not meet our criteria for a continuity/discontinuity analysis, and both sites have been relegated to the chapter "Other Sites."

LACONIA:

Survey work by Waterhouse and Hope Simpson has yielded much information on the transitional period MH/LH (Waterhouse and Hope Simpson 1960, 1961). Architectural remains have been attested, however, only in the Menelaïon near Sparta and at Aghios Stephanos, and since neither meets our criteria for analysis, they have been consigned to the chapter "Other Sites."

MESSENIA:

Publications by McDonald, Hope Simpson and the Minnesota expedition have provided much useful survey information on the transitional period MH/LH I in Messenia (McDonald and Hope Simpson 1961, 1964, 1969 and McDonald and Rapp 1972). Significant architectural remains have been attested in Pylos (McDonald and Rapp 1972:264 # 1), Koukounara (ibid.:270 # 35), Methoni (ibid.:278 # 80), Nichoria (ibid.:280 # 100), Peristeria (ibid.:290 # 200) and Malthi (ibid.:296 # 222). Our criteria for a continuity/discontinuity analysis were only useful in the case of Pylos, and all other sites can be found in our chapter "Other Sites."

As mentioned above (see infra p. 15), McDonald's and Hope Simpson's observations on the occupation of the south-west Peloponnese deserve our attention. For a large number of settlements their survey assembled elementary evidence such as "dura-

22

tion of occupation" and "beginning and end of occupation." This collected evidence has been arranged and discussed by period in chapter 8 of the Minnesota publication.

For the EH and MH periods, we know the following: there are 22 certain EH settlements and 58 certain MH settlements or cemeteries, 44 of which were established on previously unbuilt ground (McDonald and Rapp 1972:131, 133). From this total of 22 certain EH and 58 certain MH sites, we can draw several conclusions. Firstly, if 44 of the 58 MH sites were newly founded, 14 (58-44) were already occupied during the EH period. Secondly, if 14 of the 22 certain EH settlements continued to be occupied during MH, 8 (22-14) must have been abandoned before the start of the MH period. We can say, therefore, that about 30% of certain EH settlements were abandoned and 76% of certain MH settlements or cemeteries were founded on previously unbuilt ground.

We can evaluate the MH and LH periods with the same simple, arithmetical method: there are 58 certain MH settlements or cemeteries and 60 Early Mycenaean (LH I-III A) sites, 23 of which were already occupied during MH (McDonald and Rapp 1972: 133, 137-8). Again some useful conclusions: firstly, if 23 of 60 LH I-III A sites were already occupied during MH, then 37 (60-23) must have been founded on previously unbuilt ground. Secondly, if 23 of the 58 MH settlements continued to be occupied during LH, then 35 (58-23) must have been abandoned before LH I. We can say, therefore, that 60% of certain MH settlements or cemeteries were abandoned and that just over 60% of LH I-III A sites were founded on previously unbuilt ground.

To summarize: during EH/MH 30% of known sites were abandoned and 76% of sites were newly established, while for the period MH/LH the figures are in each case about 60%. On the basis of survey information put forward by the Minnesota expedition, there are obviously no grounds for assuming continuity of occupation of the area in general during these two periods.

The lack of specificity in data used (no subdivisions into EH I, II and III having been made) makes it impossible to draw any conclusions on continuity/discontinuity (McDonald and Rapp 1972: 133, 136, 138, 141).

PYLOS:

A rich find of MH/LH I architectural remains has come to light

23

on the hill Epano Englianos and at its foot (Blegen and Rawson 1966:31, 33). For this study we have used information on the northeastern gateway and wall and on the Belvedere area of the acropolis (Blegen and others 1973:4-7, 18-23). Elsewhere on the acropolis are other traces of MH architecture, but these have either been disturbed, not precisely dated or not correlated with distinctive pottery (Blegen and others 1973:8-18, 24-47 passim). The same difficulties occur in assessing finds in the Lower Town (Blegen and others 1973:47-68 passim).

The northeastern gateway and wall were erected on stereo at the beginning of LH. "In its preserved part the wall has a minimum thickness of 1.40 m. and it seems to have been laid on a flattish cutting in stereo" (Blegen and others 1973:6, cf. 4). "So far as could be determined, however, the Early Mycenaean ware, principally of Late Helladic I, (...) must mark the period when the gateway had been built and was in use" (Blegen and others 1973: 7).

Walls laid on stereo and datable to LH I were also found in square W 38, the Belvedere area: "The survival of these early walls lying in the hollow, worn or sunk in stereo, extending across the plateau of the acropolis, gives ground to conclude that the hill in Late Helladic I was occupied by houses" (Blegen and others 1973: 23).

Two interpretations of this information are possible: either all previous constructions were destroyed to make room for this LH I gateway and wall, or the LH I architecture was constructed on virgin ground. Both cases would meet our criteria for conclusive evidence of discontinuity.

The walls laid on stereo in area W 38 also give evidence of discontinuity, for they too were either newly built or built to replace constructions of an earlier period.

Conclusion: New building or destruction of older building in the period LH I are conclusive evidence of discontinuity of occupation.

Late MH/LH I: 4

ELIS:

Publications by Sperling, Meyer, McDonald and Hope Simpson and the Minnesota expedition provide much survey information on Elis during the transitional period late MH/LH I (Sperling 1942,

24

Meyer 1957, McDonald and Hope Simpson 1961, 1964, 1969 and McDonald and Rapp 1972:300-8, register nrs. 244-332). Many of the sites discussed in McDonald and Rapp 1972 are in Elis, and general conclusions on continuity/discontinuity of occupation in the southwest Peloponnese are equally valid for Elis (see above p. 22-3).

Significant architectural remains have been attested in Káto Samikon (McDonald and Rapp 1972:302 # 302), Epitálion (ibid.: 302 # 303), Olympia Altis (ibid.:304 # 315), Olympia New Museum (ibid.:306 # 321), Miraka (ibid.:306 # 323) and Chlemutsi. In no case has it been possible to analyze for continuity/ discontinuity, and all these sites will be found in our chapter "Other Sites."

ACHAIA:

The architectural remains attested on the hill Drakotrypa near Kataraktis do not meet our criteria for analysis, and this site has been relegated to our chapter "Other Sites."

ATTICA AND AEGINA:

Significant architectural remains have been attested in Athens (Acropolis and the Boulevard of Dionysius the Areopagite), Thorikos, Brauron, Marathon, Eleusis and near the Aphrodite Temple on Aegina. With the exception of Eleusis, these sites do not allow a continuity/discontinuity analysis and will be found in the chapter "Other Sites."

ELEUSIS:

Important architectural remains from the late MH and LH I periods have been excavated on the south face of the acropolis of Eleusis. Stratified architectural remains and correlated distinctive pottery were found in the area of house H.

Partly under floor level in house H and partly outside it lie the foundations of house Z (Mylonas 1932:fig. pp. 4-5). The excavator dates house H to LH I by means of a Vapheio cup found on the floor of the contemporary house I (Mylonas 1932:29ff; cf. 113 fig. 90). The walls of house H rest in part on rock and in part on a leveling surface from the Minyan period (Mylonas 1932:31).

The underlying house Z, where Yellow Minyan pottery was found, must have been in use during late MH (Mylonas 1932:27-8,

25

77). House walls remaining from H do not correspond completely
with those of Z. The building of house H with its differing floor
plan, over house Z, which was still in use in late MH, is evidence of
discontinuity. Even stronger evidence is the layer of ash between
late MH and LH niveaux over the entire area (Mylonas 1932:11,
14, 159). Therefore we can accept the excavator's conclusions:
"Ὁ τελευταῖος μινύειος συνοικισμὸς κατεστράφη διὰ πυρὸς εὐθὺς
δαμέσως ... ἐπὶ τῶν ἰσοπεδωθέντων ἐρειπίων αὐτοῦ ἰδρύθη τὸ
ὑστεροελλαδικὸν I χωρίον" (Mylonas 1932:159).

Conclusion: Signs of destruction and subsequent rebuilding to a
different architectural plan are conclusive evidence of discontinuity.

Late MH/LH I: 4

BOEOTIA:

Architectural remains have been found at Thebes and Eutresis
(see above p. 17). Though dates have been established for both
sites, neither lends itself to a continuity/discontinuity analysis,
and they may be found in our chapter "Other Sites."

PHOCIS:

Significant architectural remains from the transitional period
MH/LH have been found in Krisa and in Kirrha. We have been able
to analyze Kirrha with our criteria, and Krisa will be found in
chapter "Other Sites."

KIRRHA:

The Magoula at Kirrha has yielded architectural remains from
the transitional period late MH/LH I. It has not always been possible to check the conclusions which the excavators put forward
in their report, so that these must sometimes be accepted at face
value.

Exactly when MH ended and LH I began is not clear at a first
reading of the report. Few architectural remains have been preserved
from HM IIIa, but the period is more clearly fixed by ceramic
evidence: "Le minyen gris devient de plus en plus rare tandis qu'
apparaissent les premiers tessons minyens jaunes" (Dor and others
1960:32). HM IIIb, on the other hand, can be dated by extensive
architectural remains. Pottery of this period differs from that of
HM IIIa in that it is predominantly Yellow Minyan in combination
with "pre-Mycenaean" ceramic ware (Dor and others 1960:32, 91).

The architecture of HR I retained the traditions of HM IIIb (Dor and others 1960:35), and HR I ceramics, as Yellow Minyan disappeared, were dominated by pre-Mycenaean forms (Dor and others 1960:96).

The designation HM IIIb suggests that the period lay at the end of the Middle Helladic. Pottery attributed to HM IIIb, however, includes several Vapheio cups, a form which is known to occur at the beginning of LH (Dor and others 1960:93, nos. 63, 64; cf. Dickinson 1974:115 fig. 3). It would seem to be sensible and even necessary to examine other pottery attributed to HM IIIb.

The excavators not having used Furumark's typological categories, we have used the illustrations provided to determine whether the so-called HM IIIb pottery could be dated LH I. Indeterminate illustrations aside (Dor and others 1960:91-3, nrs. 61-2), we can definitely assign to LH I the Vapheio cup shown (Dor and others 1960:91-3, nr. 63, Pl. LII, compare Dickinson 1974: 115, fig. 3), and nrs. 56, 57, 58 and 67 as well (Dor and others 1960:91-3), compare Furumark shapenumbers 211, 212, 218 or 237 and shapenumber 27). Numbers 59 and 60 (Dor and others 1960:91-3) are definitely MH pottery (Frödin and Persson 1938: 291, fig. 200 nr. 1). Following the rule that a newer element, in this case LH I pottery, dates the older, here MH pottery (see above p. 21), we may assume that Kirrha HM IIIb is contemporary with the beginning of the LH I period (compare also Dor and others 1960:100-2).

One consequence of this conclusion is that the HM IIIa period in Kirrha lay at the end of MH. The equivalence seems to be borne out by the presence of Yellow Minyan ware during this period (cf. Buck 1964:282). HR I, then was a continuation of LH I, an assumption borne out by HR I pottery (Dor and others 1960:96-7, nrs. 68 to 73).

Taken together the facts indicate that the transition late MH/ LH I in Kirrha spans the end of HM IIIa and the beginning of HM IIIb. The excavators report a layer of burnt debris under HM IIIb remains and, here and there, substantial walls overlaying scanty HM IIIa remains (Dor and others 1960:32). On the accompanying section drawings one can see these HM IIIb walls in all five pits and the meager HM IIIa remains in pits 2 and 5 (Dor and others 1960:Pl. IV).

Conclusion: Layers of burnt debris and a new pattern of re-

27

building are conclusive evidence of discontinuity of occupation during the transitional period late MH/LH I.

Late MH/LH I: 4

EUBOEA:

Survey work by Sackett and others (1966) revealed a large number of possible MH/LH sites. Significant architectural remains have come to light near Manika and Lefkandi, but in neither case was a continuity/discontinuity analysis possible, and they have been relegated to our chapter "Other Sites."

OTHER SITES EH/MH

ARGOLID:

Prosymna, the Argive Heraeum: EH strata and remains of houses
have been attested, but in the absence of distinctive pottery sherds
it has not been possible to date more exactly (Blegen 1937:13-5).
MH material was found overlying a layer of ash, which itself lay
immediately over bedrock (Blegen 1937:17).

Dendra near Midea: On the matter of EH/MH architecture, the
excavator simply comments: "Since only comparatively few Early
Helladic remains have been discovered on the acropolis of Midea,
it seems probable that building was concentrated during this
period mainly on this part of the slope adjoining the plain" (Persson
1942:20).

Synoro: Remains of houses reported to have been found here are
of possible EH and MH date (Döhl 1971:197).

Kandia: A preliminary account reports: "The first was the fortified
hill of Kandia, ...; HM houses were found below some of them and
a few EH III vases" (Dunbabin 1944:82).

Phlius: "Definite evidence for occupation begins in Early Helladic
II when an apparently large settlement extended over the site both
in the plain and on the acropolis. Here some rubble house walls
were associated with the pottery, but no buildings were cleared ...
No sherds were found which could be attributed to either EH III
or the Middle Helladic period ..." (Biers 1969:457). Further details
were not included in this publication.

Spetsai: Part of a house, lying some centimeters under modern
surface, was excavated and dated by associated EH II pottery:
"῞Οτι πιθανῶς ἡ μορφὴ αὐτοῦ ἦτο ≪ μεγαροειδὴς ≫ φαίνεται ἐκ

29

τῶν λειψάνων τῶν ἐγκαρσίων τοίχων Καὶ ἐντος τοῦ μικροῦ ὑπολειφθέντος τμήματος τοῦ ἐσωτερικοῦ τοῦ οἰκήματος αὐτοῦ καὶ ἐπὶ τῶν λίθων τοῦ πρὸ αὐτοῦ λιθοστρώτου (προφανῶς ≪ αὐλῆς ≫) εὑρέθησαν πλήρη σχεδὸν ἢ εὐχερῶς συμπληρούμενα πρωτοελλαδικὰ ἀγγεῖα, διὰ τῶν ὁποίων χρονολογεῖται τὸ κτίσμα εἰς τὴν αὐτὴν γενικωτέραν ὑποπερίοδον (IIE II). Εἰς τὸ ἀνώτατον μέρος τῆς ἐπιχώσεως, σχεδὸν δὲ ἐπὶ τῆς ἐπιφανείας, παρετηρήθησαν ὄστρακα μυκηναϊκῶν ἀγγείων"(Theochares 1971:88). Mycenaean pottery recovered from the stratum immediately overlying an EH II house led the excavator to the conclusion that Spetsai was abandoned at the end of the EH II period: "Καθ' ὅσον γνωρίζομεν σήμερον, ὁ Πρωτοελλαδικὸς II οἰκισμὸς τῆς Ἁγίας Μαρίνας ἠρημώθη (ἄγνωστον ἐκ ποίας αἰτίας) περὶ τὸ τέλος τῆς περίοδου, διεκόπη δὲ ἡ περαιτέρω συνέχεια, πιθανῶς ἐπὶ πολλοὺς αἰῶνας." (Theochares 1971:92). The preliminary character of this publication makes inclusion of this site in our study inadvisable.

CORINTHIA:

Corinth: Architectural remains have also not been revealed by more recent excavating (Williams 1973:1; Williams 1972:144-5). The absence of EH III pottery, noted by Caskey (Caskey 1960: 300), has been corroborated by this later work.

Goniá: Vestiges of EH and MH houses have been attested, but associated pottery is lacking (Blegen 1930:59).

Perachora: Evidence of occupation during the EH period is recognized (Payne 1940:29). EH II pottery, such as "sauceboats," has been recovered, but EH III pottery is totally lacking.

Prehistoric settlement near *LakeVouliagmeni, Perachora*: Fossey comments on this settlement: "Without further excavation it is not possible to establish the date and nature of the first settlement(s) on the site" (Fossey 1969:69). Only very short accounts of supplementary work on this site are available (Catling 1972/3: 8-9; Michaud 1973:268).

Korakou: It has not been possible to decide whether the layer of burnt debris overlying the EH strata, of which Blegen speaks (Blegen 1921:2), is datable to the end of EH II or of EH III (Blegen

30

1921:122; Caskey 1960:301).

ARCADIA:

Pheneos: Deposits indicating occupation during MH, and containing architectural remains, have been discovered north of the Asklepieion. Not distinct, however, is whether we are dealing here with a new MH settlement on previously unbuilt ground (criterium 4), since the virgin soil below has not been reached (Protonotariou-Deilaki 1965:159; Megaw 1965/66:8; Schachermeyr 1971:406).

LACONIA:

Pavlo Petri: Architectural remains and pottery from EH and MH were found here, but it has not as yet been possible to acquire information on the stratified layers of this underwater settlement (Harding 1969:139).

MESSENIA:

Malthi: Its excavator, Valmin, tells us that the EH settlement at Malthi (Dorion II) is covered with a layer of ash (Valmin 1938:52, 400-1). No distinctive EH II or EH III ware has been recovered from EH levels (Valmin 1938:275-85). Doubts concerning Valmin's pottery classifications and his stratigraphic claims (McDonald and Rapp 1972:132) make it inadvisable to draw any conclusions here.

Nichoria: It would appear that the earliest settlement on the ridge near Nichoria was founded during the MH period. One cannot accept this conclusion, however, as the preliminary excavation report does not make clear whether the very earliest MH material was found directly over bedrock or not (McDonald 1972:229, 230, 237, 271).

Pylos: Evidence of occupation has been found outside the citadel: "Within the area of the aloni were the partial structural remains of a Bronze Age settlement that was probably transitional between Early and Middle Helladic. One cannot be more specific than that, for the pottery evidence was very scanty ..." (Blegen 1973:220).

Akovitika: There is reason to suppose that both Megaron A and Megaron B in Akovitika were built and abandoned during the period EH II (McDonald and Rapp 1972:290 # 151; Themelis 1970:303-

31

11; Papathanasopoulos 1970:177-9; Michaud 1971:892; Karagiorga
1971:126-9; Catling 1971/72:10). The preliminary nature of these
publications makes inclusion of this site inadvisable.

ELIS:

Olympia Altis: Two occupation layers of prehistoric date, separated
by a layer of sand, were discovered by Dörpfeld in the area of the
Altis (Dörpfeld 1935:66 Abb. 1, Taf. 6). The uppermost of these
two layers, itself overlaid by sand (Dörpfeld 1935:80), contained
the foundations of a number of apsidal houses (Herrmann 1962:
16 Abb. 2). Since the pottery found on site (Herrmann 1962:24
Nt. 97) does not allow us to date these apsidal houses definitely
to either EH III or early MH, we cannot include the site in our
study.

Olympia New Museum: The most comprehensive report notes:
"Εἰς τὸ κατώτατον στρῶμα, ὀλίγον ἄνωθεν τοῦ φυσικοῦ ἐδάφους
καὶ εἰς βάθος 2.50 μ., εὑρέθησαν εἰς τὴν ἑτέραν τῶν τάφρων
ὄστρακα μεσοελλαδικὰ καὶ ὑπολείμματα θεμελίων κτηρίων (Πίν.
116β)" (Yalouris 1960:126).

ACHAIA:

Åström's survey of Mycenaean sites in Achaia also records EH/MH
remains (Åström 1964). Possible settlements are Xeriko (Åström
1964:109), Drakotrýpa (Åström 1964:103) and Aigion (Schachermeyr 1971:393), but in no case does the nature of the remains
allow us to venture a continuity/discontinuity analysis.

ATTICA AND AEGINA:

Brauron: After exploratory work by Papadimitriou on the acropolis
at Brauron, excavation revealed, among other finds, some MH
houses (Papadimitriou 1949:83, 1961). It is not possible to
establish whether these houses were built in early MH, as it is not
clear which pottery has been recovered from each level (Papadimitriou 1961:77-78). Elsewhere on the hill EH remains have been
recovered (Papadimitriou 1961:79). Whether a new settlement was
founded in the neighbourhood of this EH settlement in the beginning of the MH period is not clear from available evidence, and
supplementary excavations have not elucidated this point (Daux
1963:712).

32

Thorikos: Evidence of MH occupation and architectural remains have been found on Velatouri hill. It was not possible for the excavators either to establish a relationship between the various walls (Mussche and others 1965:20) or to obtain a more or less complete floor plan for any one house. More exact dating of any one MH house remains, therefore, out of the question (Mussche and others 1965:10, 15, 20-4).

Marathon: EH and MH architectural remains have been found near "Plasi" (Marinatos 1970:153-4).

Rafina: The remains of a fortified settlement of the EH period have been excavated on the coast near Rafina (esp. Theochares 1955, 1956, 1960), and an EH III house has been discovered on the "acropolis" in the same neighbourhood (Theochares 1960: 116). With regard to the coastal settlement, EH, MH and LH occupation have all been attested (Theochares 1956:109-10). Although Theochares observed that the last two phases of the EH period could be established with the help of pottery evidence, his classification unfortunately is not based on the Lerna classification and must be revised (Theochares 1956:112-8). According to him, house A and the contemporaneous house Δ were lived in during the EH III period (Theochares 1956:108), but a closer examination of the pottery found in house A shows it to comprise mainly "sauceboats" and Lerna III bowls (Theochares 1955:142 Fig. 10). This permits the correction that houses A and Δ were inhabited during the EH II rather than the EH III period (compare Aghios Kosmas etc.). Since the stratigraphy above this EH II stratum is completely disturbed, a continuity/discontinuity analysis for the transitional periods EH II/EH III and EH III/early MH is not possible.

Askitario: Theochares reports that the EH settlement here was abandoned or destroyed at the end of EH, most probably after the EH III phase (Theochares 1957:104). According to him, the excavated houses A, B, Γ, Δ, E, Z and H all belong to the EH III phase, but the pottery found on site forces the same correction as that made for Rafina, namely: Askitario EH III = Lerna III = EH II (Theochares 1957:105, 108-9; 1960:114). Ambiguities in the stratigraphy make it very difficult to say with any certainty

33

whether Askitario was indeed abandoned at the end of EH II.

Aegina: Pre-Myceaean architectural remains have been attested on the site of the Aphrodite temple. In the absence of other data, it is not possible to date more accurately (Staïs 1895:235-64; Harland 1925:20-1; Wolters 1925; Welter 1938:11, 101). Supplementary excavations have not yielded further useful information about the EH/MH transitional period (Walter 1967, 1971).

BOEOTIA:

Thebes: EH and MH architectural remains and pottery have been found, but exact dating is lacking (Symeonoglou 1973:12-3).

Lithares: Report of the excavations near Lithares notes signs of burning in the upper levels of the EH period, but this evidence was too scanty for the excavators to assume that the EH settlement was destroyed (Spyropoulos 1969:36, later Spyropoulos and Tzavella-Evjen 1973:371-5).

PHOCIS:

Krisa: Traces of an MH settlement have been found at Krisa. Its excavators argue that the settlement was established on virgin ground sometime after the beginning of the MH period (Jannoray and Van Effenterre 1937:300-1). This dating is based on the absence of Black Minyan ware (Jannoray and Van Effenterre 1938: 111). But the presence or absence of Black Minyan is no longer a good basis for dating. A large quantity of Grey Minyan (Jannoray and Van Effenterre 1938:113) and some Mattpainted coarse ware (Jannoray and Van Effenterre 1938:121) are also present, so that it is possible to assume that the settlement at Krisa was founded in EH III (Howell 1973:78-9) or early MH (Buck 1964:280-1). But which dating is correct is unclear. As the excavators have not reported whether the earliest architectural remains are associated with Grey Minyan alone or with Grey Minyan combined with Mattpainted coarse ware (Jannoray and Van Effenterre 1937:303-4, 306, 308), it is not possible to be more precise.

EUBOEA:

Lefkandi (Xeropolis): Architectural remains have been found in trench CC at levels designated EH and MH (Popham and Sackett

34

1968:6). The earliest architectural remains from phase 1 are datable to a period contemporary with EH III (Popham and Sackett 1968:8), so that the transition EH II/EH III must be located beneath phase 1, but on this no useful information has been provided by Popham and Sackett.

Transition EH III/early MH must be looked for above phase 1. As the earliest Grey Minyan ware was recovered from phase 2 (Popham and Sackett 1968:8), while the earliest Mattpainted coarse ware came from phase 5, the transition EH III/early MH must lie somewhere between. Over phase 2, where signs of building were lacking, traces of houses were again found in phases 3 and 4, but it is not possible on the basis of this evidence to determine during which of these intervening phases Lefkandi made the transition EH III/early MH. On this question the excavators make no comments.

Dickinson suggests that the transition at Lefkandi from phase 2 to 3 is coeval with the transition at Lerna from IV to V (Dickinson 1977:20).

THESSALY:

Although one speaks of architectural remains from the Early Bronze Age on sites near present-day Volos (Theochares 1964 and 1966), Thessaly cannot be included in this study, for it is questionable whether we have to do here with an EH culture. The earliest Bronze Age pottery, which the excavator terms contemporary with EH pottery, exhibits strong differences. Important types, such as "sauceboats," are lacking (Theochares 1964:123) or, if present and attested, are assumed to be imported material (Theochares 1966:65). In general, it would appear that the Early Bronze Age culture in Thessaly had its own historical development (Howell 1973:80) and must be distinguished from the EH period in Greece. All this implies that it would be an error to include evidence of cultural transformations during the Bronze Age in Thessaly in a study of the Helladic period.

OTHER SITES MH/LH

ARGOLID:

Mycenae: MH architectural remains have come to light near the West House (late MH/LH I), near the Great Ramp and near the House of Sphinxes. Reports in all three cases are too scanty to allow a continuity/discontinuity analysis (Schachermeyr 1971: 405; for a listing of all reports see Schachermeyr 1974:4).

Tiryns: A fairly large house was found in the southwest part of Trench F in the lower city at Tiryns, but precise details for dating the niveaux are lacking. On the history of the house, the excavators comment: "Es kann nicht ausgeschlossen werden, dass auf den Fundamentmauern eines Hauses, das in der Übergangszeit vom Mittelhelladikum zum Späthelladikum durch Brand zerstört wurde, in frühmykenischer Zeit wieder ein Haus aufgeführt worden ist. Noch in SH I/II ging dieses zweite Gebäude mit seinen starken und sorgfältigen Fundamentmauern zugrunde; darüber wurden andere frühmykenische Bauten errichtet ..." (Gercke and Hiesel 1971:8).

Lerna: For the transitional period late MH/LH I only very rough data are available: "Toward the close of the Middle Bronze Age burials on the site itself increase in number, though in the highest strata still preserved house walls and floors continue to occupy most of the area. Ultimately the place was used for mighty shaft graves, ..." (Caskey 1956:173, compare Caskey 1958:144).

Asine: LH I material overlying MH material has only been discovered in the southern part of the Lower Town (Frödin and Persson 1938:295), providing too little data to draw any conclusions. A closer study of LH I pottery found at Asine has not provided more relevant information (Alin 1968:87-8).

CORINTHIA:

Zygouries: MH architectural remains were not dated (Blegen 1928: 28), despite the fact that Yellow Minyan could be attested (Blegen 1928:125-6). The excavators report: "In the late Helladic Period, as already mentioned above, the settlement apparently descended the hill and spread out over the low ground to the east and west" (Blegen 1928:135), but on what grounds they chose to date this removal of the site to the LH period is not clear.

Korakou: MH architectural remains attested for the eastern portion of the hill at Korakou could not be associated with the Yellow Minyan and Polychrome Mattpainted pottery also found there (Blegen 1921:18-9, 28-30, 76-9). LH I pottery was also excavated but again could not be associated with architectural finds (Blegen 1921:36-44).

Gonia: Both MH and LH architectural remains were found, but the report does not provide any information on dating (Blegen 1930:59).

Nemea: Though there appears to be a possibility of relating remains of houses found here to the transitional period late MH/LH I, the information published to date is still too scanty (Blegen 1927:436-7).

ARCADIA:

Asea: The abandonment of Asea during the MH period is not relevant to this study, as it has been definitely established that it did not take place at the end of that period (Holmberg 1944:20, 90, 180).

Pheneos: The excavators have labelled the architectural remains found here above the MH niveaux simply as "Mycenaean" (Proto-notariou-Deïlaki 1965:159).

LACONIA:

Menelaïon: Houses and pottery from the LH period mentioned by Waterhouse (1965:170) are not in the excavator's report (Dawkins 1909-10).

Aghios Stephanos: Since the excavations carried out by Taylour, there is information available over the occupation of this site in the late MH/LH I period. The most important finds were in areas A, Δ and B. There seems to have been a short break in occupation of area A at the end of MH (Taylour 1972:240), but verification is not possible on the basis of information provided. Abandonment of area Δ at the end of MH is also assumed. As the houses excavated in this area are all dated early MH (Taylour 1972:244), and there are no houses here from the end of MH, we cannot accept Taylour's assumptions.

In area B clearly stratified architectural remains were uncovered but could not be definitely dated by the excavators: "The pottery associated with these different walls and floors was not very distinctive, Mycenaean patterned wares being rarely found" (Taylour 1972:255). Even more unfortunate is the fact that, for the distinctive pottery such as Yellow Minyan and an LH I Vapheio cup found in area B, the exact positions of these important finds are not given (Taylour 1972:257-8, HS 99, HS 101). Reports on more recent excavations have not been able to elucidate the situation (Catling 1973-4:15-6).

MESSENIA:
Koukounara: On the hill 'Katarraki" near Koukounara, remains of dwellings, including an apsis-type megaron, were uncovered. The excavators believe these structures should be dated early LH. There is no information about niveaux underlying these dwellings, so that whether they were built on virgin soil or on an MH stratum cannot be established (Ergon 1958:151; 1959:117-8).

Methoni: Remains of what might have been a MH dwelling were found near a MH altar on "Nisikouli." Correlated pottery has been dated to the end of the MH, though neither Yellow Minyan nor Polychrome Mattpainted were found. The absence of strata later than MH points to an abandonment of the site at the end of the MH period (Choremis 1969:12-4).

Nichoria: Although both late MH and LH I material have come to light here, the stratigraphy of the architectural remains from these periods is not reported. The excavators believe that one can speak of a displacement of the settlement during the period MH/LH

38

(McDonald 1972:234, 237, 257-8; McDonald and others 1975: 136).

Malthi Dorion: A rich find of architectural remains has been uncovered here. Phenomena of interest to us are 1. restoration of a MH circuit wall during LH; 2. occupation of MH houses during LH; 3. rebuilding of MH houses during LH; and 4. construction of new houses during LH. On point one it must be noted that the restoration of the circuit wall has not been more exactly dated (Valmin 1938:23, 169). Concerning point two it can be said that a large number of MH houses were inhabited continuously from late MH to LH I (Valmin 38:77-169). On the third point the excavator remarks that rebuilding of MH houses C5, C14-17 and B1 almost definitely occured during LH I (Valmin 1938:170-3), while on point four he notes that the construction of new LH houses cannot be more precisely dated than LH III (Valmin 1938:173-85). Altogether the information pertinent to points two and three would appear to justify the conclusion that, despite traces of discontinuity, one could speak here of continuity of occupation during late MH/LH I. Unfortunately, serious doubts concerning the stratigraphic claims of the excavators (see above p. 31) make such a conclusion premature.

Peristeria: Near Peristeria the remains of a dwelling, the so-called "East House" have been found. This house had a "Vapheio cup" on the floor and a cistburial under the floor. According to our view (see above page 21), the floor and therefore also the burial must be dated to LHI times. The cutting through by the (later) tholos tomb does not, of course, change the date of the floor and the burial. As nothing is told about the levels underneath the floor of the house, conclusions pertinent to the transition late MH/LHI here cannot be drawn (Marinatos 1961-2:102 and Schachermeyr 1971:408-9).

ELIS:

Káto Samikon: While we know that Dörpfeld found Mycenaean architectural remains here, the excavator's report was never published (Meyer 1957:76).

Epitálion: A house found here was dated by its excavator (Themelis

39

1968) as LH; McDonald and Hope Simpson prefer the dating LH III (McDonald and Hope Simpson 1969:129).

Olympia: Mycenaean sherds have been recovered from several places in the Olympia area. LH architectural remains are totally lacking until now. MH architectural remains have been excavated in the Altis and near the New Museum (Herrmann 1962:23 ff; McDonald and Rapp 1972:304-6 passim).

Altis: Dörpfeld found a number of apsidal houses under a layer of sand in the Altis of Olympia. Associated pottery provided a rough dating of MH (Dörpfeld 1935:102, figs. 10, 12; Herrmann 1962: 24). Whether these houses were abandoned and covered by sand at the end of MH could not be determined (Dörpfeld 1935:102), nor could a date be established for the so-called younger apsidal houses built over this layer of sand. It is not even clear if these younger houses are prehistoric (Dörpfeld 1935:90-4). Conclusions such as abandonment of the site at the end of MH or new construction during LH are certainly not justified.

New Museum: It was not possible to date the abandonment of the MH house found here more precisely (Yalouris 1960:126; cf. above p. 32).

Miraka: Architectural remains were uncovered on the hill which Dörpfeld thought to be "Pisa." Correlated pottery allows a dating of MH, but there is no further information (Dörpfeld 1935:273-5; tables 22, 23; Sperling 1942:83-4).

Chlemutsi: At point A along the base of the circuit wall of the medieval castle at Chlemutsi, architectural traces have been found in a MH stratum (Servais 1964:13, fig. 4). Stones that must have comprised part of a house wall were found immediately above virgin wall ground. A large Mattpainted jar found on site dates house wall and stratum to the MH period. The layer of ash which covers much of this MH niveau could not be more precisely dated (Servais 1961:158, 1964:32), so that conclusions useful to this study are not possible.

ACHAIA:

Drakotrypa: House walls and MH and LH pottery have come to light here. Ålin believes himself justified in dating the settlement to the Late Mycenaean period (Ålin 1964:65).

ATTICA AND AEGINA:

Athens Acropolis: MH and LH I architectural remains have been found on the Acropolis, but no details have been published concerning the MH walls there (Iakovidis 1962:52). On the basis of the original excavation reports, we believe that the "house" which Iakovidis dated LH I can only be dated more loosely between EH and LH II because of the associated pottery (Iakovidis 1962:69-70; Holland 1924:155). Dating this "house" LH I because it is not apsidal in form, as Holland suggests (1924:156 note 2), is no longer a defensible opinion.

Athens Boulevard of *Dionysios the Aeropagite*: Foundations of two MH houses have been excavated south of the Boulevard. One of them, House Θ, was built on virgin soil. No other clues to date either the building or the abandonment of these houses more exactly have been given (Dondas 1961-2:85-6).

Thorikos: At the end of the last century, excavators uncovered architectural remains from the Mycenaean and pre-Mycenaean periods on the summit of the Velatouri hill near Thorikos (Staïs 1893:15-6; 1895:223, 226). Later excavations by a Belgian team have not provided more information on Mycenaean remains, though some details have been published on MH architectural finds. Remains of MH houses were found directly under a building of the Geometric period (Mussche and other 1967:20-4), but the absence of material which leads itself to more exact dating makes any conclusions about whether or when these houses were abandoned impossible.

Brauron: Relevant to our study is the report by Papadimitriou in the Praktika for 1956. The remains of two rooms were found on the acropolis at Brauron and were consigned by their excavator to the MH period. Within the walls of these rooms three distinct floor levels, one above the other, were uncovered, but pottery associated with each successive layer has not been reported. Near these rooms

41

both late MH and LH I-II pottery were found in a disturbed stratigraphy (Papadimitriou 1961:79-80), so it is not possible to speak definitely of continuity of occupation during the transition period MH/LH I.

Marathon: An MH house has been uncovered on the summit of the hill "Plasi," but details of the finds have not been published (Marinatos 1970:154).

Aegina: MH architectural remains have been discovered, but no details are available (Walter 1967, 1971; see also page 34). Other reports tell us of an LH settlement built on ruins, but here too precise details are unavailable (Staïs 1895:248; Buschor 1926: 121).

BOEOTIA:

Thebes: Helladic Thebes is known to us from reports on a number of very small excavations (Symeonoglou 1973:11). During the excavation of "The House of Kadmos" and "Oedipus Street 14," MH and LH architectural remains came to light. Under the actual "House of Kadmos" even older architectural remains were found which could stem from the MH or early LH periods (Keramopoullos 1909:64, 106), but later discussion has not elucidated the situation (Symeonoglou 1973:72ff).

Architectural remains which could be dated late MH were found during the excavation of "Oedipus Street 14" (Symeonoglou 1973: 13). Moreover the excavator tells of buildings from the earlier phase of the Myceaean period (Symeonoglou 1973:15). Unfortunately, none of this information is clear enough to warrant a conclusion as to continuity/discontinuity for this site.

Eutresis: A house found on the hill at Eutresis can be dated to LH I by correlated pottery. As there is no useful information concerning the possibility of underlying levels (Goldman 1931:64-6), it is impossible to draw any conclusions.

PHOCIS:

Krisa: The excavators' report speaks of a distinct layer of burnt debris which can be dated to the transition period MH/LH: "Un incendie, suivi d'un abandon partiel du site, marque la séparation

42

des deux époques mésohelladique et mycénienne. En effet, certains endroits de la fouille, où la stratigraphie est assez nette, montrent une couche de terre d'une dizaine de centimètres entre les cendres qui recouvrent l'état helladique moyen et les fondations mycéniennes, ce qui correspond à une différence de 0 M. 30 à 0 M. 40 entre le sol HM et le sol HR" (Jannoray and Van Effenterre 1937: 315). This layer of ash is important to our study only if it can be established that it was laid down between late MH and LH I constructions.

As definitely LH I construction the report lists room a in ensemble E, room g in ensemble F and room h in ensemble G (Jannoray and Van Effenterre 1937:315 note 3, 318-9, 322).

Room a/E was dated LH I on the basis of an amphoriscus found in the contemporaneous grave number 27 (Jannoray and Van Effenterre 1937:315 note 3, 311 note 1; Lerat and Jannoray 1936:143 fig. 7,7; cf. Jannoray and Van Effenterre 1938:133 note 39). On the basis of Furumark's work, this amphoriscus must be dated to the period LH III rather than LH I (Furumark shapenumber 38).

Of the pottery found in room g/F, inventory numbers 6132, 6123 and 6104 are illustrated and discussed (Jannoray and Van Effenterre 1937:318, Jannoray and Van Effenterre 1938: nrs. 27, 38, 40). Number 6132 may possible be LH I (Furumark shapenumber 268 or 269, but with an extraneous ear), 6104 may be LH I but is more likely to be LH III (Furumark shapenumber 158, 159, 160 or 161) and number 6123 comes definitely from the LH III period (Furumark shapenumber 58, 59, PU 59 or 60).

Of the pottery found in room h/G, inventory numbers 6068 and 6133 are shown (Jannoray and Van Effenterre 1938:nrs. 34, 37). Neither vase fits typologically into the LH I period: number 6068 is a vase of the type Furumark shapenumber 264 or 265 (LH IIIA) and 6133 corresponds to shapenumber 128, thus is also an LH III type.

In the light of these corrections, the dating of these rooms to LH I is no longer defensible. Too much of the pottery found here comes from a later period.

Evidence of destruction and/or abandonment of late MH houses at Krisa has provided the following clues: MH house foundations which can be correlated with Yellow Minyan ware were found in Bâtiments C and D (Jannoray and Van Effenterre 1937:306-8),

43

but at neither site were traces of destruction or abandonment discerned.

Having considered all these points, it is not possible to say that the layer of burnt debris referred to can be dated to the transitional period late MH/LH I: the so-called LH I buildings are probably of a later date, and above MH buildings no signs of burning were found.

EUBOEA:

Manika: see above, page 19.

Lefkandi: There are traces of discontinuity in the occupation of the Xeropolis settlement during the transitional period late MH/ LH I. One abandoned house can definitely be dated late MH (phase 6) by the Polychrome Mattpainted pottery found there (Popham and Sackett 1968:10). Furthermore, excavators found an LH I grave cut transversely through the floor of this late MH house (Popham and Sackett 1968:10, fig. 10: Furumark shape-number 254, 263), so that its abandonment and the obvious fact that it was no longer used as a dwelling can be taken to indicate discontinuity. As information on levels immediately overlying phase 6 is not available, any further conclusions are unjustifiable.

CONCLUSION

Having arrived at the end of our study, we would like to summarize the course of our investigation. Our aim has been to analyze certain archaeological phenomena for clues to continuity and discontinuity in mainland Greek settlements during the period ± 2000 to 1600 BC. We began by establishing which phenomena could be accepted as reliable indices of different levels of (dis)continuity. These indices were then applied to information available on 54 settlements at which architectural remains have been found. Most of these settlements proved to be useless for our purposes, as essential information on stratigraphy and the exact site of particular styles of pottery were either not reported or were so indistinctly or incompletely presented that they could only be analyzed with the greatest difficulty. But where necessary information was available, it proved relatively simple to arrive at (dis)continuity values, and at no time during our study was it necessary to revise our four-point scale of criteria.

Results of our analysis by settlement can be found in table 2. The table also shows what we assess the average discontinuity value for each period to be. Table 3 is a graph of our analysis by settlement by period. The curve for EH II/EH III shows a high level of discontinuity, with lower scores for Berbati, Eutresis and Kirrha. Based on a smaller number of sites, the curve for EH III/ early MH shows a number of lower scores, namely for Lerna and Kirrha.

The curve for late MH/LH I includes, oddly, no score lower than four, so that all four sites included indicate the maximum level of discontinuity, an obvious contrast to the curves for EH II/EH III and EH III/early MH.

Our conclusion must be that discontinuity dominated the scene during all three transitional periods, though its level at any one site and the number of sites where it could be ascertained may vary. Since our study has shown that discontinuity of settlement can

45

fairly certainly be assumed circa 2000 and circa 1600 BC, we believe that an appreciable level of immigration may equally certainly be assumed.

What is the significance of this conclusion for the discussion surrounding the arrival of the Greeks on the Greek mainland? We believe that one cannot doubt that immigration occurred both around 2000 BC and around 1600 BC. This has long been accepted for the earlier period, but to date most specialists have rejected the idea of immigration around 1600 BC. We should like, therefore, to consider our evidence for this latter period more closely.

Examination of the architectural material assigned to this period and its interpretation indicate in many cases that the stratigraphy was indistinct or had been disturbed. For this reason very few useful sites have been recorded for the late MH/LH I period. During our study we were struck by the inclination of several interpreters to see disturbed stratigraphy as a sign of continuity. This is, we believe, an unfair assumption. A disturbed stratigraphy is nothing more than evidence of disturbance and points neither to continuity nor discontinuity. Where continuity of settlement really did occur, the evidence is obvious enough.

Two kinds of settlements of the late MH/LH I period were available to us for analysis: those with an indistinct or disturbed stratigraphy and those at which the stratigraphy was untouched and readable. In every case the last category indicated discontinuity.

We do not maintain that this study provides definitive proof of either discontinuity of settlement or immigration around 1600 BC. We do, however, maintain that it is no longer possible to postulate continuity of settlement during this period without first contradicting our arguments. Nor will it be possible to base such a postulate on archaeological evidence which we have proved here is unreliable. While we cannot go into all the complex arguments for continuity around 1600 BC, it is possible to indicate some perspectives for further study which arise when discontinuity rather than continuity is accepted.

Assuming that a significant level of immigration did indeed occur around 1600 BC, traces of two distinct cultures should be found. Immigrants carried their own culture to the new land where the original population continued its own traditions. At those places where the two met traces of both cultures will appear side by side, as well as evidence of their eventually influencing and altering one another.

This view fits better with attested archaeological evidence for the period around 1600 BC than does that of a "higher" culture spontaneously evolving from a simpler indigenous tradition. No evidence of such an evolution can be attributed to the period. On the contrary, one finds both MH and Aegean pottery at the relevant sites, and graves which tell the same story of old and new forms coexisting.

The possibility of immigration and the introduction of new forms would be well worth consideration in the study of the chronology of the period. We have pointed out that local MH pottery is easily distinguished from imported Aegean and LH I pottery, but chronological tables for the period do not as yet reflect this. The traditional view has been that the end of the Middle Helladic merged smoothly into the Late Helladic I period which followed. When Aegean pottery, which strongly resembles later LH I forms, is found in upper MH strata together with MH pottery, this assumption is at first glance justified. Introduce the idea of discontinuity, however, and the appearance of imported Aegean pottery is seen to mark the beginning of something new. The continued existence of the old in no way changes the picture (see our example, page 21, of the television set in the old farm house).

Of course it is possible to keep the idea of continuity around 1600 BC artificially alive by refusing to admit this interpretation of mixed finds of MH and imported Aegean pottery in MH strata. Postulating that this evidence marks a new period could bring a much needed clarity, and unbelievable devices such as "typical" LH I Vapheiocups already used in late MH times would no longer be either necessary or possible.

Perhaps the greatest advantage in accepting the discontinuity theory is that it makes a range of new questions possible: What precisely are the characteristics of the old and new cultures? In which areas did the carriers of the new culture concentrate themselves? Where did the old traditions hold out the longest? At what stage did old and new finally merge completely? Is it possible to establish whether the Mycenaeans dominated the local inhabitants by force?

These are only a few possible areas of inquiry, and further research will show that some questions will have to be reformulated. We believe that new questions must be proposed for archaeological research into Mycenaean civilization, if we are not to bog down in a dead-ended controversy over the yes or no of (dis)continuity around 1600 BC.

APPENDIX

SIMILAR FEATURES IN THE ARCHITECTURE OF TROY AND MALTHI DORION

Reading the literature on the question of the cultural and ethnical identity of the pre-Greek people (see above pages 2-3), one finds time and again references to connections, similarities or points of comparison between the cultures of North West Anatolia and the Greek mainland during the Middle Bronze Age (French 1973:51-3; Howell 1973:86-8; Caskey 1973:140).

This is especially so in recent architectural studies of walled settlements (Best and Yadin 1973:24 note 33). Although the number of excavated and attested examples is very small (see "Other Sites" and Cook 1973), and one is limited to Troy VI and Dorion IV (Malthi), it would be worthwhile to compare the architecture of these two cities.

We wish to compare the characteristic features of such settlements during a given period, in this case the Middle Bronze Age. Is the distinctive style of enclosing walls, towers and houses, which we observe in one settlement, also to be seen in the other? Since we confine ourselves to a typological examination, the charge of "unreliable stratigraphic claims" leveled at the excavator of Dorion (see above page 31) becomes less important.

Comparing these walled cities, we have made a distinction between defensive architecture and town planning. An analysis of defensive architecture would include the ground plan which the fortification followed, its construction, its gates and the presence of towers along its length. These are considered by Niki Scoufopoulos to be the chief points in a study of defensive architecture (Scoufopoulos 1971:14). Our analysis of town planning concentrated on the placement of houses within the walled area.

1. Ground plan

The fortification of Troy VI, which curves around the south side of the city, is still well preserved. Though its segments can be distinguished from one another, the wall is not composed of straight, angled sections. The fortification of Dorion IV can be followed in its entirety on its inner surface. The wall describes "gentle curves" around the city (Valmin 1938:16, general plan), and here too each slightly curved section contributes to the whole curved ground plan.

2. Construction

The fortification of Troy VI is composed of inner and outer walls with a fill between (Blegen and others 1953:84-9, 91-4, 102-4, 105-7, fig. 16). One noticeable detail is that the stones are of different sizes laid in almost regular courses. Care has been taken to avoid placing vertical joints directly above each other (Blegen and others 1953:ibid., figs. 9, 19, 38, 68, 78).[1] Blegen remarks: "The core of the wall was ... a solid fill of rubble ..." (Blegen and others 1953:91).

Describing the fortification of Dorion IV, Valmin writes: "The faces of the wall were built of larger, better-joined blocks, the interior between them being filled up with stones of varying sizes thrown down in confusion" (Valmin 1938:16-17, general plan). His illustrations show that both inner and outer walls were constructed of different sized stones and that vertical joints nowhere

---

1. Characteristic features of the wall of Troy VI are the so-called "offsets" and the "batter" (Blegen and others 1953:81-113). The "offsets" seem to have had a decorative function (Dörpfeld 1902:120), while the "batter" found in the fortification — and in the retaining wall of house VI M — was a structural necessity. At the time of its building, the ground niveau inside the wall was approximately four meters higher than that outside, so that the fortification had also to work as a retaining wall (Blegen and others 1953: 166-7).
The wall of Dorion IV lacks both "offsets" and "batter." It did not need to work as a retaining wall, as there was no appreciable difference in ground niveaux within and without the fortification (Valmin 1938; general plan, section A-B). These differences between Troy VI and Dorion IV (in decoration and retaining function), which can partly be explained by local conditions, do not invalidate the similarities noted in our study.

lie above each other (Valmin 1938:34 fig. 10. On plate VIII 5, 6, IX 2, the fortification is visible in the background).

3. Gates

At Troy VI we have examined separately 1) the gates and 2) other construction, such as secondary walls and towers, in their immediate vicinity. Basically, a gate is a break in the fortification of a city. One noticeable feature of the gates of Troy is that they do not simply interrupt an extension of a single line. Rather, there is a shift in orientation of the walls on either side of the openings; at gate VI T, for example, the shift is about one meter between the inner surface of section 3 on one side of the opening and that of section 4 on the other (Blegen and others 1953;figs. 449-51). This shift in orientation exists more or less at all gates with the exception of the postern gate VI R (Blegen and others 1953:81-113, fig. 446, 447, 451, 472, 503).

2) Secondary walls can be seen inside gate VI S (Blegen and others 1953:333, figs. 447, 472) and gate VI U (Dörpfeld 1902:135ff, fig. 46) and outside gate VI V (Blegen and others 1953:104-5, figs. 447, 503, 504). Towers VI k and VI i were built near gate VI T. Tower VI k is a massive, rectangular widening of the actual fortification (Blegen and others 1953:93, fig. 451), while VI i is a smaller, rectangular annex to the outer surface of the wall (Blegen and others 1953:95-100, figs. 447-52).

1) Three attested gates of Dorion IV are B 18, D 53 and D 8, while D 77 can be classified as a postern gate (Valmin 1938:17-20). Shifts in the orientation of the walls on either side of the gates are quite obvious at B 18 and D 8, barely noticeable at D 53 and non-existant at D 77 (Valmin 1938: general plan).

2) A secondary wall can be seen inside D 8 and D 77 as well as inside B 18 (Valmin 1938:17-20, general plan). The rectangular widening of the walls at gates D 53 and B 18 can be viewed as massive towers of the type found at tower VI k in Troy (Valmin 1938: general plan). There are no towers at the gates of Dorion of the annex type, such as at VI i in Troy.

Aside from the tower-like section 1 of the fortification of Troy VI, which protects the northeast area of the city, tower VI h, a small, rectangular annex to the outer surface of the wall, is the only other tower not situated at a gate. There is, therefore, no system of regularly-spaced towers along the length of the fortification.

51

Though no complete towers remain along the defensive wall of Dorion IV, there are some indications that they existed. D 30 (Valmin 1938:22, general plan) may have been the side wall of a small, square annex-like tower on the outer surface of the fortification, and one could assume the same construction for D 1 (Valmin 1938:20-2, general plan).

TOWN PLANNING

Most of the houses in Troy VI were large, rectangular, detached buildings, sometimes with several rooms (Blegen and others 1953: 115ff, figs. 446, 447). This is very different from Dorion IV, where houses were built in clusters of attached rooms (Valmin 1938: general plan).

If one assumes with Blegen that there is a strong case for cultural continuity between Troy VI and Troy VIIa, it is reasonable to compare architectural phenomena in Dorion IV with similar phenomena in Troy VIIa. Several square rooms were built near gate VI S on the inner surface of the fortification of Troy VI, which continued to be used for Troy VIIa (Blegen and others 1958:107-19, fig. 338). "Magazines" built along the western wall of Dorion IV between B 28 and B 88 are similar in size and form to rooms VII a, VII β, VII γ, VII ϵ, and VII ζ in Troy VIIa (Valmin 1938:140-58, general plan).

CONCLUSION

In Troy VI we find the following combination of architectural details: a curved fortification wall composed of a series of segments, an occasional shift in orientation of walls on either side of gates and the presence of both massive and annex-like towers.

In Dorion IV we find: a curved fortification wall composed of segments, an occasional shift in orientation of walls on either side of gates and the presence of massive towers.

Given these similarities, and the fact that the same method was used to construct the fortification of Troy VI and Dorion IV, we conclude that these two cases represent a specific type of fortified

52

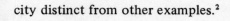
city distinct from other examples.[2]

2. Comparisons can be made by studying the ground plan of Aegina: the curved wall, massive towers and magazines (Welter 1938:fig. 9). It would be useful to consider whether the architecture of Iron Age Old Smyrna continued some of the traditional features of Bronze Age architecture in the Troad; curved walls, massive towers, a shift in orientation at gates and a secondary wall are all to be found there (Cook 1958-9:15 fig. 3).

53

Table 1

LIST OF SITES CONSIDERED (CF. MAP 1)

		EH/MH	MH/LH
ARGOLID			
1	Mycenae		x
2	Tiryns	x	x
3	Argive Heraeum	x	
4	Synoro	x	
5	Dendra	x	
6	Argos	x	x
7	Lerna	x	x
8	Asine	x	x
9	Berbati	x	
10	Kandia	x	
11	Phlius	x	
12	Spetsai	x	
CORINTHIA			
13	Corinth	x	
14	Korakou	x	x
15	Gonia	x	x
16	Perachora	x	
17	Lake Vouliagmeni	x	
18	Zygouries	x	x
19	Nemea		x
ARCADIA			
20	Asea	x	x
21	Pheneos	x	x
LACONIA			
22	Menelaïon		x
23	Pavlo Petri	x	x
24	Aghios Stephanos	x	x
MESSENIA			
25	Malthi	x	x
26	Nichoria	x	x
27	Akovitika	x	
28	Pylos		x

55

		EH/MH	MH/LH
29	Koukounara		x
30	Methoni		x
31	Peristeria		x
ELIS			
32	Olympia	x	x
33	Kato Samikon		x
34	Epitalion		x
35	Miraka		x
36	Chlemutsi		x
ACHAIA			
37	Drakotrypa		x
ATTICA AND AEGINA			
38	Athens		x
39	Aghios Kosmas	x	
40	Brauron	x	x
41	Thorikos	x	x
42	Rafina	x	
43	Askitario	x	
44	Marathon	x	x
45	Eleusis	x	x
46	Aegina	x	x
BOEOTIA			
47	Thebes	x	x
48	Orchomenos	x	
49	Chaeronea	x	
50	Lithares	x	
51	Eutresis	x	x
PHOCIS			
52	Kirrha	x	x
53	Krisa	x	x
EUBOIA			
54	Lefkandi	x	x

Table 2

LIST OF SITES ANALYZED (CF. TABLE 3, MAP 2)

	EHII/EHIII	EHIII/early MH	late MH/LHI
TIRYNS (2)	4	–	–
ARGOS (6)	–	4	4
LERNA (7)	4	1	–
ASINE (8)	4	–	–
BERBATI (9)	2	4	–
ZYGOURIES (18)	4	–	–
ASEA (20)	4	–	–
AGHIOS STEPHANOS (24)	4	4	–
PYLOS (28)	–	–	4
AGHIOS KOSMAS (39)	4	–	–
ELEUSIS (45)	–	4	4
EUTRESIS (51)	1	4	–
KIRRHA (52)	2	3	4
	33:10=3,3	24:7=3,42	16:4=4

1 = Conclusive evidence of continuous occupation.
2 = Evidence of continuity of occupation with traces of discontinuity.
3 = Evidence of discontinuity of occupation with traces of continuity.
4 = Conclusive evidence of discontinuity of occupation.

Table 3

GRAPH OF SITES ANALYZED

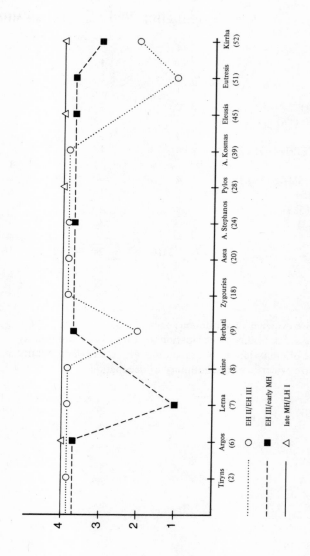

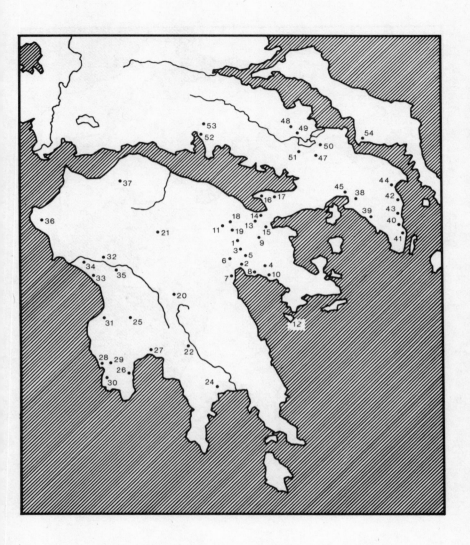

Map 1
SITES CONSIDERED
(The numbers refer to the sites of table 1)

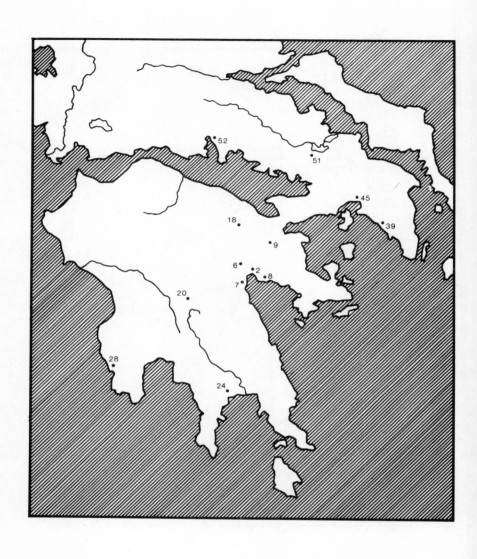

Map 2
SITES ANALYZED
(cf. table 1, 2 and 3)

60

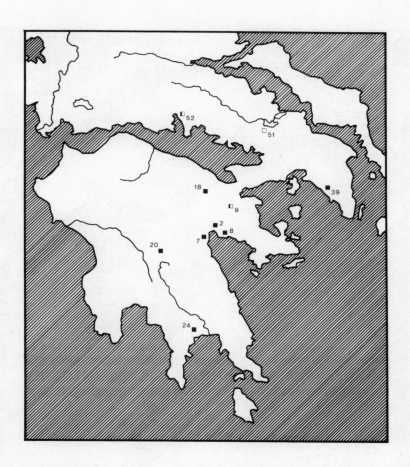

□   1   conclusive evidence of continuous occupation

◨   2   evidence of continuity of occupation with traces of discontinuity

◧   3   evidence of discontinuity with traces of continuity

■   4   conclusive evidence of discontinuity of occupation

Map 3
TRANSITIONAL PERIOD EH II/EH III

61

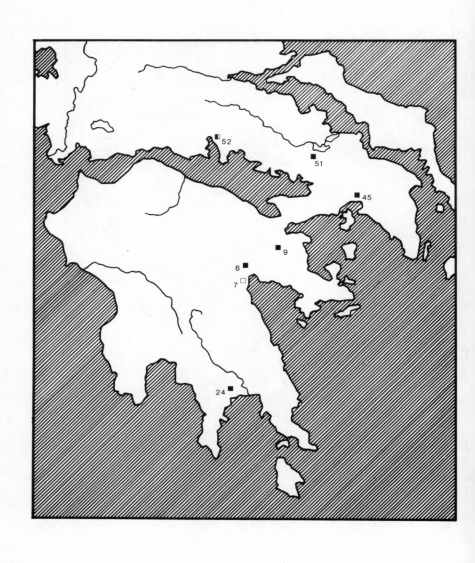

Map 4
TRANSITIONAL PERIOD EH III/EARLY MH

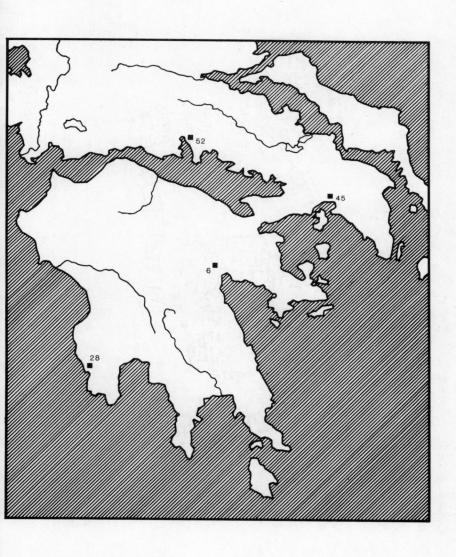

Map 5
TRANSITIONAL PERIOD LATE MH/LH I

63

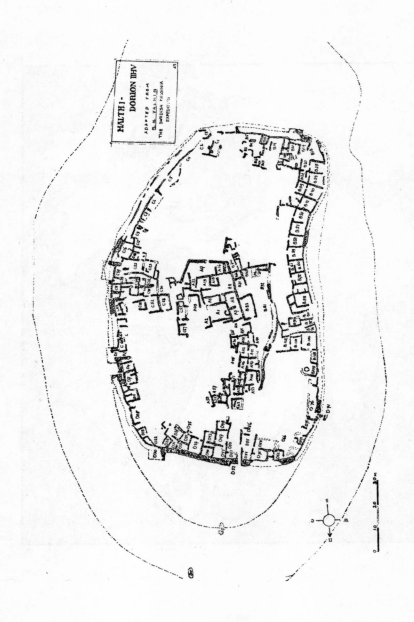

Fig. 9
PLAN OF MALTHI DORION III - IV

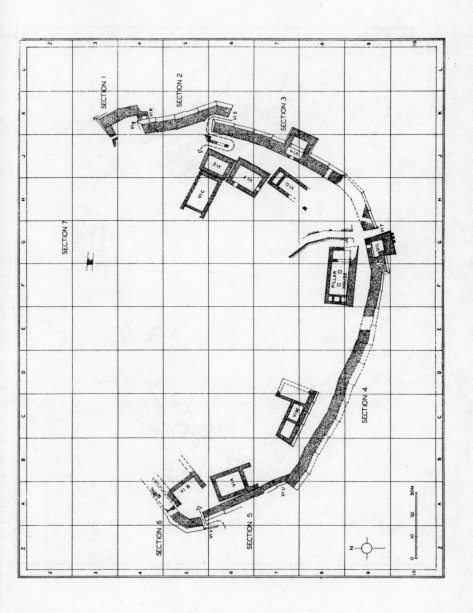

Fig. 10
PLAN OF TROY VI

65

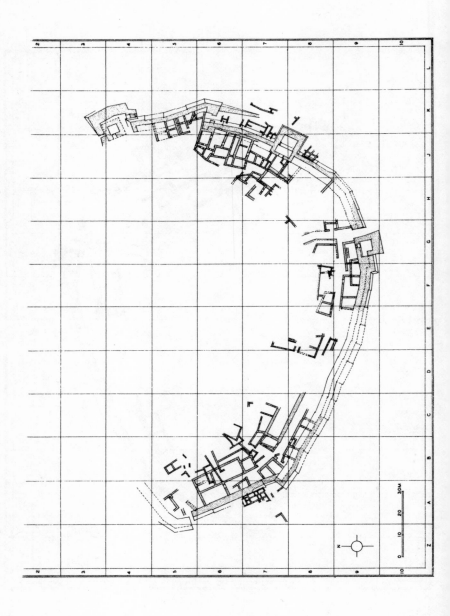

Fig. 11
PLAN OF TROY VII

66

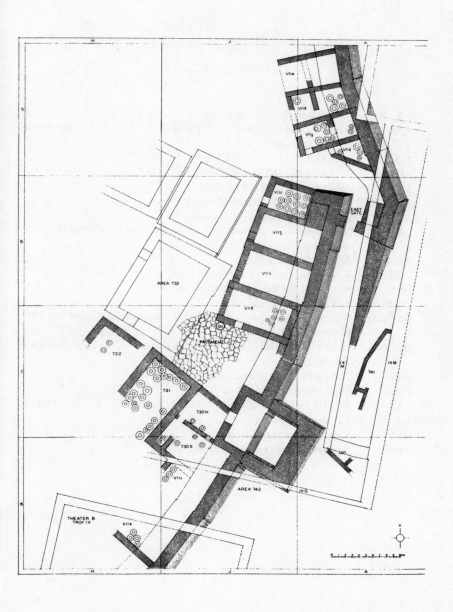

Fig. 12
PART OF TROY VIIa NEAR GATE VI S

LIST OF ABBREVIATIONS

AA	Archäologische Anzeiger.
AAA	ΑΡΧΑΙΟΛΟΓΙΚΗ ΑΝΑΛΕΚΤΑ ΕΞ ΑΘΗΝΩΝ, Athens Annals of Archaeology
AD	ΑΡΧΑΙΟΛΟΓΙΚΟΝ ΔΕΛΤΙΟΝ.
AD Chr.	ΑΡΧΑΙΟΛΟΓΙΚΟΝ ΔΕΛΤΙΟΝ ΧΡΟΝΙΚΑ.'
AE	ΑΡΧΑΙΟΛΟΓΙΚΗ ΕΦΗΜΕΡΙΣ.'
AEM	ΑΡΧΕΙΟΝ ΕΥΒΟΙΚΩΝ ΜΕΛΕΤΩΝ..
AJA	American Journal of Archaeology.
AM	Mitteilungen des Deutschen Archäologischen Instituts. Athenische Abteilung.
AR	Archaeological Reports.
BCH	Bulletin de Correspondance Hellénique.
BSA	Annual of the British School at Athens.
Ergon	ΕΡΓΟΝ.
Gnomon	Gnomon. Kritische Zeitschrift für die gesamte klassische Altertumswissenschaft.
Hesperia	Hesperia. Journal of the American School of Classical Studies at Athens.
JHS	The Journal of Hellenic Studies.
OAth	Opuscula Atheniensia.
PAE	ΠΡΑΚΤΙΚΑ ΤΗΣ ΕΝ ΑΘΗΝΑΙΣ ΑΡΧΑΙΟΛΟΓΙΚΗΕΤΑΙΡΕΙΑΣ
RA	Revue Archéologique.
REG	Revue des Etudes Grecques.
SMA	Studies in Mediterranean Archaeology.

REFERENCES

Ålin, P.   1968   "Unpublished Mycenaean Sherds from Asine".
                          O.Ath., 8:87-105.
—   1962   *Das Ende der Mykenischen Fundstatten auf
                          dem griechischen Festland.* Lund.
Åström, P.   1964   "Mycenaean pottery from the region of Aigion,
                          with a list of prehistoric sites in Achaia". *O.Ath*,
                          5:96-100.
Bengtson, H.   1969²   *Griechische Geschichte – von der Anfängen bis in
                          die römische Kaiserzeit (Sonderausgabe).* München.
Best, J.G.P. and Yadin, Y., 1973   *The Arrival of the Greeks.* Amsterdam.
Biers, W.R.   1969   "Excavations at Phlius, 1924, the prehistoric
                          deposits". *Hesperia* 38.443-458.
Blegen, C.W.   1921   *Korakou – A prehistoric Settlement near Corinth.*
                          Boston and New York.
—   1927   "Excavations at Nemea 1926". *AJA*, 31.421-40.
—   1928   *Zygouries – a prehistoric settlement in the valley
                          of Cleonae.* Cambridge (Mass.).
—   1930   "Goniá". *Metropolitan Museum Studies* III:55-80.
—   1937   *Prosymna – the Helladic settlement preceding the
                          Argive Heraeum.* Cambridge.
—   1963   *Troy and the Trojans.* London.
Blegen, C.W. and Rawson, M., 1966   *The Palace of Nestor at Pylos in
                          Western Messenia I.* Princeton.
Blegen, C.W. and others, 1953   *Troy – the sixth settlement.* Princeton
                          (N.J.).
Blegen, C.W. and others, 1958   *The palace of Nestor at Pylos in Western
                          Messenia, III.* Princeton.
Bommelaer, J.F. and Grandjean, Y., 1971   "Travaux de l'école française en
                          1970". *BCH*, 95:736-70.
Buck, R.J.   1964   "Middle Helladic Mattpainted pottery". *Hesperia*
                          33:231-313.
Bulle, H.   1907   *Orchomenos I – Die älteren Ansiedlungsge-
                          schichten.* München.
Buschor, E.   1926   "Nachrichten. Ausgrabungen des Deutschen Ar-
                          chäologischen Instituts in Griechenland". *Gnomon*,
                          II:120-3.

Buschor, E.   1927   "Vom Amyklaion". *AM* 52:1-64.

Caskey, J.L.   1956   "Excavations at Lerna, 1955". *Hesperia*, 25:147-73.

— —   1958   "Excavations at Lerna, 1957". *Hesperia*, 27:125-44.

— —   1960   "The Early Helladic Period in the Argolid". *Hesperia*, 29:283-303.

— —   1962   "Kirrha. Etude de préhistoire phocidienne (rev.)". *AJA*, 46:211.

— —   1966   "Houses of the Fourth Settlement at Lerna". *Kharistirion eis Anasiasion K. Orlandhou III (Bibliothiki tis en Athinais Arkhailogikis Etaireias 58)*:144-52.

— —   1973   "Greece and the Aegean Islands in the Middle Bronze Age". CAH II 1:117-40.

Caskey, J.L. and E.G., 1960   "The earliest Settlements at Eutresis supplementary Excavations, 1958". *Hesperia*, 29:126-67.

Catling, H.W.   1971-1972   "Archaeology in Greece, 1971-72". *AR*, 18:3-26.

— —   1972-1973   "Archaeology in Greece, 1972-73". *AR*, 19:3-32.

— —   1973-1974   "Archaeology in Greece, 1973-74". *AR*, 20:3-41.

Choremis, A.K.   1969   "ΜΕ ΒΩΜΟΣ ΕΙΣ «ΝΗΣΑΚΟΥΛΙ» ΜΕΘΩΝΗΣ, *AAA*, 2:10-4.

Coldstream, J.N. and others, 1972   *Kythera*. London.

Cook, J.M.   1973   "Bronze Age Sites in the Troad". *Bronze Age Migrations in the Aegean (Archaeological and Linguistic problems in Greek prehistory, ed. by R.A. Crossland and Ann Birchall)* London:37-40.

— —   1958-59   "Old Smyrna, 1948-1951". *BSA*, 53-54:1-34.

Croissant, F.   1972   "Rapports sur les travaux de l'école française en 1971". *BCH*, 96:883-6.

Daux, G.   1956   "Chronique des fouilles en 1955". *BCH*, 80:219-432.

— —   1959   "Chronique des fouilles en 1958". *BCH*, 83:567-793.

— —   1965   "Chronique des Fouilles et découvertes archéologiques en Grèce en 1962". *BCH*, 91:623-890.

— —   1969   "Chronique des fouilles et des travaux de l'école française d'Athènes en 1968". *BCH*, 93:955-1062.

Dawkins, R.M.   1909-10   "Laconia. Excavations at Sparta, 1910". *BSA*, 16:4-11.

Deshayes, J.   1966   *Argos – les fouilles de la Deiras*. Paris.

Dickinson,O.T.P.K.,1974 "The definition of Late Helladic I". *BSA*, 69.109-20.
—— 1977 *The Origins of Mycenaean Civilisation (SMA*, XLIX)
Doehl, H. 1971 "Die prähistorische Besiedlung von Synoro". *Tiryns Forschungen und Berichte* V. Mainz am Rhein.
Dörpfeld, W. 1902 *Troja und Ilion*. Athens.
—— 1935 *Alt-Olympia*. Berlin.
Dondas, G. 1961-62 "ΑΝΑΣΚΑΦΗ ΟΙΚΟΠΕΔΟΥ ΑΓΓΕΛΟΠΟΥΛΟΥ" *AD*, 17:83-95.
Dor, L. and others, 1960 *Kirrha. Etude de préhistoire phocidienne*. Paris.
Dunbabin, T.J. 1944 "Archaeology in Greece, 1939-45". *JHS*.
Fossey, J.M. 1969 "The prehistoric settlement by Lake Vouliagmeni, Perachora". *BSA*, 64:53-69.
French, D.H. 1973 "Migrations and 'Minyan' pottery in western Anatolia and the Aegean". *Bronze Age Migrations in the Aegean (Archaeological and linguistic problems in Greek prehistory, ed. by R.A. Crossland and Ann Birchall)*. London:51-7.
Frödin, O and Persson, A.W., 1938 *Asine — Results of the Swedish Excavations 1922-1930*. Stockholm.
Gercke, P. and Hiesel, G., 1971 *"Grabungen in der Unterstadt von Tiryns von 1884 bis 1929". Tiryns Forschungen und Berichte V*. Mainz am Rhein.
Goldman, H. 1931 *Excavations at Eutresis in Boeotia*. Cambridge (Mass).
Grossmann, P. and Schäfer, J., 1971 "Tiryns: Unterburg, Grabungen 1965". *Tiryns Forschungen und Berichte V*. Mainz am Rhein.
Harding, A., Cadogan, G. and Howell, R., 1969 "Pavlopetri, an underwater Bronze Age town in Laconia". *BSA*, 64:113-42.
Harland, J.P. 1925 *Prehistoric Aegina*. Paris.
Hermann, H.V. 1962 "Zur ältesten Geschichte von Olympia". *AM*, 77. 3-34.
Holland, L.B. 1924 "Erechtheum papers II". *AJA*, 28:142-69.
Holmberg, E.J. 1944 *The Swedish excavations at Asea in Arcadia*. Lund.
Hope Simpson,R. 1965 A Gazetteer and Atlas of Mycenaean Sites (Bulletin of the Institute of Classical Studies, Suppl. no. 16, London).
Howell, R.J. 1973 "The origins of the Middle Helladic culture". *Bronze Age Migrations in the Aegean (Archaeological and linguistic problems in Greek prehistory ed. by R.A. Crossland and Ann Birchall)*. London: 73-101.
Iakovidis, S. 1962 Η ΜΥΚΗΝΑΙΚΗ ΑΚΡΟΠΟΛΙΣ ΤΩΝ ΑΘΗΝΟΝ.

71

Jannoray, J. and Van Effenterre, H., 1937   "Fouilles de Krisa". *BCH*, 61: 299-326.
——   1938   "Fouilles de Krisa". *BCH*, 62:110-47.
Karagiorga, T.G.   1971   "AKOBITIKA". *AD*, 26:126-9.
Keramopoulos, A.D., 1909   "Η ΟΙΚΙΑ ΤΟΥ ΚΑΔΜΟΥ". *AE* 1909:57-122.
Kunze, E.   1934   *Orchomenos III - Die Keramik der frühen Bronzezeit.* München.
Lerat, L. and Jannoray, J., 1936   "Premières recherches sur l'acropole de Krisa (Phocide)". *RA 6e série*, VIII:129-45.
Marinatos, Sp.   1961-62 "ΑΝΑΣΚΑΦΑΙ ΜΥΛΟΥ". *AD* 17:101-3.
——   1970   "Further news from Marathon". *AAA*, 3:153-66.
——   1973a   *Kreta, Thera und das Mykenische Hellas.* München.
——   1973b   "The first Mycenaeans" "in Greece". *Bronze Age Migrations in the Aegean (Archaeological and linguistic problems in Greek prehistory ed by R.A. Crossland and Ann Birchall).* London:107-13.
McDonald, W.A.   1972   "Excavations at Nichoria in Messenia: 1969-71". *Hesperia*, 41:218-73.
McDonald, W.A. and Hope Simpson, R., 1961   "Prehistoric habitation in Southwestern Peloponnese". *AJA*, 65:221-60.
——   1964   "Further exploration in Southwestern Peloponnese: 1962-1963". *AJA*, 68:229-45.
——   1969   "Further explorations in Southwestern Peloponnese: 1964-1968". *AJA*, 73:123-77.
McDonald, W.A. and Rapp jr., G.R., 1972   *The Minnesota Messenia Expedition (reconstructing a Bronze Age Regional Environment).* Minneapolis.
McDonald, W.A. and others, 1975   "Excavations at Nichoria in Messenia: 1972-1973". *Hesperia*, 44:69-141.
Megaw, A.H.S.   1965/66 "Archaeology in Greece, 1965-66'. *AR*, 12:3-24.
Meyer, E.   1957   *Neue Peloponnesische Wanderungen.* Bern.
Michaud, J.P.   1971   "Chronique des fouilles et découvertes archéologiques en Grèce en 1970". *BCH*, 95:803-1067.
——   1973   "Chronique des fouilles et découvertes archéologiques en Grèce en 1972". *BCH*, 97:253-412.
——   1974   "Chronique des fouilles et découvertes archéologiques en Grèce en 1973". *BCH*, 98:579-722.
Müller, K.   1930   *Tiryns — Die Ergebnisse der Ausgrabungen des Instituts III.* Augsburg.
Mussche, H.F. and others, 1967   *Thorikos 1965 III.* Brussels.
Mylonas, G.E.   1932   ΠΡΟΙΣΤΟΡΙΚΗ ΕΛΕΥΣΙΣ. Athens.
——   1959   *Aghios Kosmas — An Early Bronze Age Settlement and Cemetery in Attica.* Princeton (N.J.).
——   1966   *Mycenae and the Mycenaean Age.* Princeton.

72

Nikopoulou, Y.   1968   "ANΑΣΚΑΦΗ ΠΡΟΙΣΤΟΡΙΚΗΣ ΚΙΡΡΑΣ". *AAA*
                            1:144-6.
Papadimitriou, I. 1949   "ANΑΣΚΑΦΑΙ ΕΝ ΒΡΑΥΡΩΝΙ ΤΗΣ ΑΤΤΙΚΗΣ"
                            PAE, 1945-48:81-90.
——   1961   "ANΑΣΚΑΦΑΙ ΕΝ ΒΡΑΥΡΩΝΙ". *PAE*, 1956.73-
                            89.
Papathanasopoulos, 1970 "AKOBITIKA ΚΑΛΑΜΑΤΑΣ". *AD*, 25.177-9.
Payne, H.   1940   *Perachora – the sanctuaries of Hera and Limenia.*
                            Oxford.
Persson, A.W.   1942   *New tombs at Dendra near Midea.* Lund.
Petrakos, V.   1973   "ANΑΣΚΑΦΗ ΕΝ ΚΙΡΡΑΙ ΚΑΤΑ ΤΟ 1972".
                            AAA, 6:70-3.
Popham, M.R. and Sackett, L.H., 1968 *Excavations at Lefkandi, Euboea*
                            1964-66. London.
Protonotariou-Deïlaki, E., 1965   "ANΑΣΚΑΦΗ ΦΕΝΕΟΥ". *AD Chr.*, 20:
                            157-9.
Sackett, L.H. and others, 1966   "Prehistoric Euboea: contributions toward
                            a survey". *BSA*, 61:33-112.
Säflund, G.   1965   *Excavations at Berbati 1936-37.* Uppsala.
Schachermeyr, F. 1968   "Zum Problem der Griechischen Einwanderung".
                            Atti e Memorie del 1e congresso internationale di
                            Micenologia Rome: 297-317.
——   1971   "Forschungsbericht zur ägäischen Frühzeit". *AA*,
                            86:387-419.
——   1974   "Forschungsbericht zur ägäischen Frühzeit". *AA*,
                            89:1-28.
Scoufopoulos, N.S., 1971 *Mycenaean Citadels (SMA, XXII).* Lund.
Servais, J.   1961   "Recherches sur le port de Cyllène". *BCH*, 85.
                            123-61.
——   1964   "Le site helladique de Khlémoutsi et l'Hyrminè
                            homérique". *BCH*, 88:9-50.
Siedentopf, H.B. 1971   "Frühhelladische Siedlungsschichten auf der Unter-
                            burg von Tiryns". *Tiryns, Forschungen und*
                            Berichte V. Mainz am Rhein.
Sotiriadis, G.   1912   "Fouilles préhistoriques en Phocide". *REG*, 25:
                            253-99.
Sperling, J.   1942   "Explorations in Elis, 1939". *AJA*, 46:77-89.
Spyropoulos, Th.G., 1969 "ΛΙΘΑΡΕΣ ΘΗΒΩΝ". *AD*, 24:28-46.
Spyropoulos, Th. and Tzavella-Evjen, H., 1973   "Lithares: An Early Hella-
                            dic settlement near Thebes". *AAA*, 6:371-5.
Staïs, V.   1893   "ANΑΣΚΑΦΑΙ ΕΝ ΘΟΡΙΚΩΙ". *PAE* 1893:12-7.
——   1895   "ΠΡΟΙΣΤΟΡΙΚΟΙ ΣΥΝΟΙΚΙΣΜΟΙ|ΕΝ ΑΤΤΙΚΗΙ
                            ΚΑΙ|ΑΙΓΙΝΗΙ". *AE*: 193-264.
Stubbings, F.H.   1973   "The rise of Mycenaean civilization". *CAH* II. 1:

627-58

Symeonoglou, S. 1973 *Kadmeia I, Mycenaean Finds from Thebes, Greece excavation at 14 Oedipusst.* (Studies in Mediterranean archaeology vol. XXXV). Göteborg.

Syriopoulos, K.T. 1964 Η ΠΡΟΙΣΤΟΡΙΑ ΤΗΣ ΠΕΛΟΠΟΝΝΗΣΕΟΥ. Athens.

— 1968 Η ΠΡΟΙΣΤΟΡΙΑ ΤΗΣ ΣΤΕΡΕΑΣ ΕΛΛΑΔΟΣ. Athens.

Taylour, W.D. 1972 "Excavations at Ayios Stephanos". *BSA* 67:205-70.

Themelis, P.G. 1968 "Thryou – Epitaliou". *AAA*, 1:201-4.

— 1970 ΠΡΩΤΟΕΛΛΑΔΙΚΟΝ ΜΕΓΑΡΟΝ ΕΙΣ ΑΚΟΒΙΤΙΚΑ ΜΕΣΣΗΝΙΑΣ". *AAA*, 3:303-11.

Theochares, D.R. 1955 "ΑΝΑΣΚΑΘΗ ΕΝ ΑΡΑΦΗΝΙ". *PAE*, 1952:129-51.

— 1956 "ΑΝΑΣΚΑΦΗ ΕΝ ΑΡΑΦΗΝΙ". *PAE*, 1953:105-18.

— 1957 "ΑΝΑΣΚΑΦΗ ΕΝ ΑΡΑΦΗΝΙ". *PAE*, 1954:104-13.

— 1959 "ΕΚ ΤΗΣ ΠΡΟΙΣΤΟΡΙΑΣ ΤΗΣ ΕΥΒΟΙΑΣ ΚΑΙ ΤΗΣ ΣΚΥΡΟΥ". *AEM*, 6:279-328.

— 1960 "ΑΝΑΣΚΑΦΗ ΕΝ ΑΡΑΦΗΝΙ". *PAE*, 1955:109-17.

— 1964 "ΑΝΑΣΚΑΦΑΙ ΕΝ ΙΩΛΚΩΙ". *PAE*, 1961:119-30.

— 1966 "ΑΝΑΣΚΑΦΑΙ ΕΝ ΙΩΛΚΩΙ". *PAE*, 1962:54-69.

— 1971 "ΑΓΙΑ ΜΑΡΙΝΑ ΣΠΕΤΣΕΩΝ". *AD Chr.* 26:84-93.

Valmin, N.M. 1938 *The Swedish Messenia expedition.* Lund.

Vermeule, E. 1972 *Greece in the Bronze Age.* Chicago, London.

Voigtländer, W. 1973 "Tiryns Unterburg-Kampagne 1972". *AAA*, 6:28-38.

Vollgraff, W. 1906 "Fouilles d'Argos". *BCH*, 30:5-45.

— 1907 "Fouilles d'Argos". *BCH*, 31:139-84.

Wace, A.J.B. and Thompson, M.S., 1912 *Prehistoric Thessaly.* Cambridge.

Walter, H. 1967 "Grabungsbericht: Akropolis von Agina". *AD Chr.*, 22:147.

— 1971 "Ausgrabung auf dem Stadhügel von Alt-Agina". *AD Chr.*, 26:61-2.

Waterhouse, H. 1956 "Prehistoric Laconia: A note". *BSA*, 51:168-71.

Waterhouse, H. and Hope Simpson, R., 1960 "Prehistoric Laconia: Part I". *BSA*, 55:67-107.

— 1961 "Prehistoric Laconia: Part II". *BSA*, 56:114-175.

Welter, G. 1938 *Aigina.* Berlin.

Williams, C.K. and Fisher, J.E., 1972   "Corinth, 1971: the Forum Area".
                                            Hesperia, 41:143-84.
——   1973   "Corinth, 1972: the Forum Area". *Hesperia*, 42:
                                            1-44.
Wolters, P.   1925   "Ausgrabungen am Aphroditetempel in Agina
                                            1924". *Gnomon*, I:46-9.
Yalouris, N.   1960   "ΑΡΧΑΙΟΤΗΤΕΣ ΗΛΕΙΑΣ ΑΧΑΙΑΣ". *AD Chr.*,
                                            16:125-6.

INDEX